Video & Online Marketing Strategies
for Wellness Professionals

UNLEASH THE POWER OF VIDEO
STAND OUT, GET SEEN & GROW

Featuring Presentation Transcripts By
Kevin Anson, Robert Gardner, Tim Cooper &
Delight Iverson

Foreword by Akbar Sheikh

Tim Cooper & Gael Wood

Global Wellness Professional Marketing
Summit Success Series

Praise from the readers of "Global Wellness Professionals Marketing Summit Success Series

"This book is an absolute must for anyone who is new (and not so new!) to marketing their business – it is a marketing bible! I started my business six months ago and truthfully have been putting posts on Facebook and spreading a few leaflets around to try and get in front of potential clients. I had no strategy – or even knew that I needed to have one! I naively thought that just telling people I was offering these services would be enough for them to book with me. The advice and knowledge these experts offer to grow your audience, which will then grow your client base, is priceless. In any business, it is vital to gain visibility in order to be successful, and this book tells you all the secrets to ensure your name gets in front of the people you need to see it. I am now far more confident I can grow my business in a much more timely manner, using the advice and suggestions from these industry leaders."

Justine Antoska
Naturally Serene Massage Therapy, UK

"Generous is the word that comes to mind after reading this book. Each presenter gave a wealth of information to improve my marketing business strategies using simple, easy and effective techniques. Many thanks and gratitude to everyone."

Ann Bell, owner
The Healing Haven, Washingtonville, NY, USA

"Wow! Great content! So many tips and step by step instruction on how to make your presence known in online videos, Google listings, Facebook Ads and more. Not only did I see how I was doing things wrong but now I have the tools to make it better. Thank you Kevin Anson, Robert Gardner, Tim Cooper & Delight Iverson!"

Laura Krieger, Massage Therapist & Instructor
Heavenly Oasis Massage Therapy

"This is an amazing book; it really helped me in my practice. There are a lot of things I would never think to use. Great Ideas..."

Regina Montalvo, LMT
Knead A Massage

Tim Cooper Education
1210/10 Fifth Avenue
Palm Beach, Queensland 4221
Australia
https://globalwellnessprofessionalsmarketingsummit.com

Video & Online Marketing Strategies for Wellness Professionals / Tim Cooper & Gael Wood —1st ed.

The Global Wellness Professionals Marketing Summit Series

Get the whole series

Success Strategies for Wellness Professionals
Achieve your goals and beat your money blocks

Are you feeling **trapped**, **stuck** and **frustrated** in your business? Feel like you're just **spinning** your wheels? These summit transcripts from Drew Elliott, Daphne Wells, and Rebecca Brumfield will provide you with the tools to get you moving forward again.

Networking & Local Marketing Strategies for Wellness Professionals
How to build valuable business relationships by connecting with your community

These summit transcripts from Marcus Bird, Andy Ramsay, Gael Wood and Felicia Brown will show you how to present yourself as the **knowledgeable** professional that you are, and **invite** clients to your practice, without sweaty palms or stumbling over your words.

For more information and links to the Kindle and Paperback editions, please visit

http://gwpms.com/summit-success-series-2018

Preface

Sharing the information that will help wellness professionals build a successful practice is a passion of mine. I will never forget the feeling of struggling in my business and wishing that somebody would just tell me what to do to turn things around!

As I discovered and tried different marketing strategies, everything changed. Not only was my business booming, but my confidence and leadership skills grew as well. This is my hope for you as well.

Do you ever wish that you could reach more people and tell them about what you do and how you can help them? Most of us know we could do that face to face.

We have an opportunity at this time to do exactly that on a much bigger scale and at very little cost. Your ideal clients are looking for solutions, and video marketing, local search engine optimization (SEO), and Facebook marketing can help them find you and feel an instant connection with you that builds trust and confidence in your skills.

The best time to start marketing your business was a year or two ago; the second-best time is right NOW! Yes, it can be scary to put yourself out there, and it can be frustrating to learn new technology, but your dreams and your clients are worth it. Imagine how you will feel a few weeks from now when you see results from creating videos, Facebook ads, and updating your SEO.

In this book, derived from selected presentations from the Global Wellness Professionals Marketing Summit, four experts in video and online marketing will take you step by step through the process of creating your video business card, marketing your business with video content, optimizing your local SEO and the best way to get started with Facebook ads on a budget.

The Global Wellness Professionals Marketing Summit has already helped thousands of wellness professionals build their businesses and get excited about marketing. Are you ready to put yourself out there, and get found online too?

Gael Wood

Gael Wood
Co-host Global Wellness Professionals Marketing Summit

Foreword

The concept of "value" is an interesting topic.

How does one give or provide value?

There are different formats to do this. The written word is good. Audio (the spoken word) is also good. But video is the best. So, you can give value in any which way you prefer. You can write articles or blog posts, you can do podcasts, or you can do videos.

The most profitable for me has absolutely been video. The reason being is that people can see who you are. They can see via your mannerisms, via your expressions, and via your tonality what you're really about. They can start building a relationship with you.

It's actually scary how good this strategy works. I mean, I've been putting out content for a little while and I put out valuable videos, or videos that provide value. I'll do Facebook Lives. My Facebook Lives give content. A lot of times, I just let people know what I did today. I simply do a Facebook Live at the end of the day. It's really cool because it keeps me accountable and people really seem to enjoy that because we do cool things every day... or, at least, we try to.

What ends up happening is this: **people buy from those they like and trust**. Not only that, but if you want to take it to a deeper level, they buy what you believe in. So, every day (or pretty much every day), I'm talking what I believe in. I'm talking about making the world a better place. I'm talking about entrepreneurship to make the world a better place. I'm talking about giving to charity. I'm talking about giving back. I'm talking about doing things ethically. And this is how you make your competition irrelevant is by showing everyone who you are.

The sad part is that most people try to be something they're not. You know, they'll see someone online, and they'll be like, "Oh, this guy's making money. Let me try to be like him!" You know everyone has the thought of making money online.

"Okay, this guy's making money online, and he's super active, so I'm going to try to be that." And they go and try to make a video, and they're super animated, like, "Oh, hey, how's it going? Oh, we've got a special sale over here!" But this approach doesn't convert or work for them because there's a disconnect; it's not natural. Others can tell that they're not authentic.

So, the craziest thing in the world that people don't realize is that the most profitable person you can be is actually yourself. Some people think to themselves, "Oh, no, dude. I'm nobody special. I'm not this big personality. No one is going to want to buy from me!" That's total nonsense.

Understand this: someone loves you (besides your mom) — a colleague, a friend, maybe your significant other. That means you're capable of being loved. Think about this concept of love for a second. It's pretty freaking wild. If you love someone, you'll do anything for them. If you have a significant other, think about what you'd do for that person. Not too long ago, that person was a total, complete stranger; yet, now, you'll literally do *anything* for them. You'd even take a bullet for them, wouldn't you? That's love. Love is strong. And someone loves you. That means you have characteristics about you; there's something about you that's lovable. And that translates online. For one person to love you, that means many people can love you... if you allow people to see *the real you*.

The first thing you must do is give yourself permission to allow others to see the real you. Only then will you profit. I can't tell you how many times people come up to me, whom I've never met in my entire life, who live in a totally different part of the country or the world, who've never met me or spoken to me, and the first time they get on the phone with me, they pay me a lofty sum to work with me one-on-one, and we're talking about a five-figure hefty investment.

They've never met me, I have a funny name, and I'm a brown-skinned, funny-looking guy… yet they buy from me. Then they tell me, "Hey, you know what, man, I can buy from anyone. You know why I buy from you? Because I resonate with you. Because you're different. Because you believe in what you're saying."

The thing is, you know, people have all these exercises for how to find their core audience, but the magical, number one, easiest way is to **just be yourself**. Because if you talk about what you believe in, if you talk about the way you like to do business, and if you talk about your "why," then people will agree with you and relate with you. People who are doing the same thing and have the same "why" will just come flocking to you. You don't have to go to them. They will come to you!

Picture this: you've got a room full of starving people and you go to the middle of the room and hold up a loaf of bread in the air. Those people are all going to come flocking to you, aren't they? Selling is like the same thing; everyone's starving for the right person to buy from. And that could be you, if give yourself permission to be yourself.

It could very easily be argued that the power of video or Facebook Lives, or just getting yourself out there, has been the number one most powerful thing in my business. You know the craziest thing? It doesn't cost anything. And listen, the best things in life are often free. Oxygen. Water. Making videos. Can you believe what I've compared it to? That's how powerful it is.

You have no reason not to try it.

Are you shy? Well, that's the world's most ridiculous excuse. Are you kidding me? If you could properly utilize video, like many other people, you can make oodles and oodles of money – and we're talking life-changing money – just from putting out quality, authentic videos.

The formula is real simple. Know your core audience like the back of your hand. Know their deepest pain points and give them content that will alleviate their pain. It's as simple as that.

One of the best ways to do this is to record your ideas. I write things down on my phone. If I see something, or if I'm just going about my day and I notice something, I just jot it down. I have a notes app on my phone, and every time I see something, I just make a note of it. I have a long list of video ideas. The ideas are easy to come up with. And if you're running short of ideas, just ask for them. Go into a relevant Facebook group and ask, "Hey, guys, what's your number one problem in _____ (whatever your niche is)?"

It's really just that simple. I mean, honestly, guys, this game is really easy. I'll be straightforward with you. The competition is lazy; they're not doing what I'm telling you to do. They gave up easily.

So, don't give up. Stick to doing three things a day that will help your business go forward.

Let me tell you something very bold. It's scientifically impossible to fail at this. I used to be homeless; it wasn't that long ago that I was living in an electrical room with no hot water. No windows. No shower. Do you understand? I was living in the back of an office building on some back road. I had a crippling anxiety disorder, I was in a toxic relationship, I was seventy pounds overweight, I had no "why," and I hated what I did for a living. I ended up in a hospital, half dead.

Success is an option. Let me repeat that. Success is an option, and you can choose it today. I suggest you do, and I suggest you start putting out videos immediately.

This is the first foreword I've ever written in my life, and it's an honor to do it for Tim and Gael because these guys really care. So, here's what I recommend. Read this book and implement it. Read a couple of pages, take notes, implement it, put the book down, implement it, then come back to the book. And you will succeed. That's the key. Don't read this book all the way through and say, "Oh, I read it in one shot, and it was a good book." That's useless. Just read a couple of pages, implement what you learn, and keep repeating that pattern. If you do, I promise you that you will succeed.

Don't forget to keep on giving along the way, either, because that's my number one secret for success. I would wish you the "best of luck," but there's no such thing, so I wish you the most enjoyable experience, and I wish and I pray that you don't give up. Only then will you succeed and, together, we can make the world a better place.

Peace.

Akbar Sheikh

To date, Akbar Sheikh has helped 7 businesses reach 7 figures. One of the businesses is a medical massage business that is now making 8 figures. To learn more about Akbar and get a free copy of his book, go to sevenfigurebook.com.

Contents

Marketing is no longer about the stuff that you make, but the stories you tell

—SETH GODIN

Introduction

You've no doubt been encouraged at some point to introduce video into your business in one form or another. After all, all the evidence is there to support the rapid trend towards video as the preferred way to consume content. Here are just a few interesting statistics –

- By 2019, global consumer Internet video traffic will account for 80% of all consumer Internet traffic (Source: SmallBizTrends)
- Facebook generates 8 billion video views on average per day (Source: Social Media Today)
- YouTube reports mobile video consumption rises 100% every year (Source: Hubspot)
- 55% of people watch videos online every day (Source: Digital Information World)

We live in very busy times. Your prospects are constantly being distracted by offers and deals. You need to get their attention fast. Give them what they want in a format that is easy to consume on the move or while they're doing other things.

But what if the thought of creating video fills you with dread? "Tim," you may say, "I'd rather have all the teeth pulled out of my head, without anesthetic before ever considering making a video!"

"I don't have any equipment," you might protest. "It costs too much. I don't have time. Is it really that important, that useful?"

1

I hear you. I wasn't always comfortable in front of the camera. That is something that has come with time and practice. And I still don't have a lot of equipment.

Let me illustrate this with one of my early experiences with video. If you had been with me the afternoon of Thursday, June 21, 2012, you would have probably been thinking to yourself, "What is this guy doing?".

You are at my home, standing in my spare bedroom. The room has been fitted out as a home clinic. My qualifications and accreditations are framed and hanging on one wall and on another wall the all too familiar muscle, nerve and skeletal charts add the finishing touches.

The air is filled with incredible aromas. Essential oils, balms, sports rubs, and liniments.

But today this room is not set up for remedial treatment. The massage table has been pushed up against a wall where the soft rays of the afternoon sun are filtering through the window providing natural light.

On top of the massage table sits a yellow plastic container, the type used for the disposal of acupuncture needles. And taped to the yellow sharps container is my Samsung S2 smartphone.

I don't have a script. I just know what I want to talk about. I sit and take a deep breath, then hit the record button on the phone and passionately share my topic for the next three and a half minutes.

Was it perfect? No. Did I have all the fancy equipment? No, I didn't even have lights or a tripod. Was I comfortable and confident in front of the camera? No. Did I know what I was doing? No

Did I share my message? Oh yeah, you bet I did.

To the casual observer, the scene would have looked comical, if not a little bizarre. A six-foot five man sitting at a massage table talking to a phone taped to a sharps container.

But it didn't matter! Those who ultimately viewed the finished video only saw me and what was in the background. They had no idea what camera I used or how it was set up. And they didn't care. They were only interested in the information and value the video delivered.

You see you don't need fancy cameras, microphones, and lights, all you need is a message and the passion for sharing it.

The following quote really resonates with me. Unfortunately, I haven't been able to identify the author, but it reads as follows

> *"Online video is the Swiss army knife of internet marketing. It really can be used all over the customer lifecycle, whether it's customer service, marketing, or even recruitment."*

Video can be used in all parts of your business. Yes, of course, it can be used to promote your business and services, your specials and promotions. But there are so many other areas where video can be employed to attract new clients and educate existing ones.

Depending on the size of your business you may consider using video as a means of induction and training staff in the operating standards and procedures.

You may even be looking at ways to generate income beyond the one-to-one, time for money treatment model. Video is a fantastic medium for creating courses for your peers or the general public.

In fact, the use of video is only limited to the imagination.

So I bet you've already guessed that I love video.

While video can be used to create great content, personal connection, and stunning promotions, it is all totally useless unless your content can be found.

The good news is there are still simple to implement strategies to get your content in front of your target market for free.

Google, for example, provides a great service to local businesses that if set up correctly will see your business listing sitting high on the first page of the Google search results. A position historically reserved for high paid ads.

Facebook is also another exciting platform that provides unprecedented insights into the behaviors, likes, dislikes and spending habits of your prospective clients. And unlike Google, it is very affordable to run successful ad campaigns.

While Facebook does make it extremely easy for you to set up ads, it's also very easy to get it wrong and spend a lot of money with little or no return.

The great news is this book has been created to help you achieve success in all these areas. We've compiled the contents of four presentations from the 2018 summit by recognized industry experts to help you understand the power of video and how you can create great videos using your smartphone.

You'll learn why it's important to get your business listed on the first page of Google and the simple steps anyone can take to get there. Finally, you'll get some insights into Facebook ads and how to create effective campaigns.

Gael and I hope you enjoy the information as much as we enjoyed compiling it for you. We also hope that you implement the strategies outlined in the book to expand your reach, increase your visibility and build the business of your dreams.

To your success

Tim Cooper
Co-host and creator of the Global Wellness Professionals Marketing Summit

Here's Your Free Gift

Exclusive to readers of the Global Wellness Professionals Marketing Summit Success Series.

If you're a solo practitioner, you are only too aware of the frustration of missing calls and client inquiries when you're in a hands-on session. Which happens 90% of the time. Right?

So what can you do?

Well, you can use a bot to take appointments details, that's what!

How to Build a Many Chat Booking Request Messenger Bot

Now you can get an 'over the shoulder' view as Kristie Melling walks you through the simple steps of automating client booking using a Facebook messenger bot.

You'll discover how to

- **Streamline** the booking request process and make the client experience more enjoyable
- Keep the client "**on the hook**" even if you're unavailable to take their call or chat in real time.
- Build a list of clients inside Facebook messenger bot that you can **message at any time**. Great for staying in touch and sending **promotions**.

Facebook Messenger is the next "big thing". Now is the time to implement this powerful business growth tool

Simply click the link below and follow the directions to access the **How to Build a Many Chat Booking Request Messenger Bot** video.

globalwellnessprofessionalsmarketingsummit.com/messenger-bot

Meet the Speakers

We are extremely honored and grateful to Kevin Anson, Robert Gardner, Tim Cooper and Delight Iverson for their valuable insights and guidance.

The material presented in this book is based on transcripts taken from their contributions to the 2018 Global Wellness Professionals Marketing Summit.

A major challenge we faced while compiling this material is transcripts prepared from live presentations read very differently to material written specifically for print. Throughout the editing process, we have endeavored to improve the flow of the content without losing the essence of the presentation.

As a result, you will occasionally encounter grammatically incorrect structures and disjointed text. We ask that you look beyond structure and focus on the message. Your persistence will be rewarded.

Kevin Anson

Kevin Anson is best known for his work producing Funnel Hacker TV for Russell Brunson.

Kevin has been producing results-driven video content since 2004. Over the course of his career, he has produced thousands of videos for companies like Inc. Magazine, Mercedes Benz, Costco, Click Funnels, Infusionsoft, Chase Bank, Bank of America, PF Chang's and many others.

Kevin has an innate passion for producing videos that convert and teaching others to do the same.

Robert Gardner

I'm Robert Gardner, and I'm a licensed massage instructor, therapist and yoga teacher in Austin, Texas. I primarily use what most consider Thai massage, yoga and pain science to help my clients and students. I've been practicing the healing arts for fifteen years and continue to push the edges of both the massage and yoga industries.

I came to this work after being in a drunk driving accident in college. I was a healthy, vibrant 22-year-old who turned into someone who was severely depressed and in pain for years with no relief due to a drunk driver. As I worked on myself and clients I blended yoga, Thai massage, and pain science into a practice I call Reboot™ 21st century manual therapy.

I believe it's the future of both the yoga and massage industries. I'm heavy on social media production, educating therapists and crushing all boxes we find ourselves in.

After authoring 700 pages of sequence manuals and what will be nine DVDs of educational content in Thai massage we began the Reboot™ Insiders Club our subscription service that documents my practice teaching therapists interactively and gives premium education to Reboot™ their own practices for $7 a month.

Tim Cooper

Tim Cooper is a Remedial Massage Therapist, coach, author, podcaster, and educator.

Before studying massage in 2003, Tim worked as a software design engineer and business analyst for over 20 years.

In 2013 Tim completed his first marketing course and fell in love with the science of marketing and social psychology.

Tim brings a unique blend of industry, technical and business knowledge to his coaching clients and students around the world.

Delight Iverson

Delight is a professional teacher and intuitive turned Facebook Ads Specialist!

She combines intuition with solid Facebook ad strategy. Her goal is to help wellness entrepreneurs become RockStars at Facebook ads so that they can shine their light all over the interwebs.

There are plenty of people out there who need and want your wonderful, magical, healing services. And Delight will show you how to reach them with Facebook ads (without breaking your budget!).

How to Create a Video Business Card

Hey, what's up? Thank you so much for reading this chapter. I am super honored and super blessed to be a part of this summit.

My name is Kevin Anson. I've been producing videos for the past 14 years. I've produced thousands of videos for some really amazing companies like Mercedes Benz, Costco, Citrix, Chase Bank, Bank of America, Infusionsoft, and ClickFunnels.

I actually produce a majority of the videos for Russell Brunson at ClickFunnels. It's just been an honor to work with those folks.

What are we going to talk about in this chapter? I want to show you how to create your own video business cards, and it's actually a lot easier than you might think. Why? Because you have a device in your pocket right now, that's actually a video camera, and that's your smartphone.

I'm going to show you, or actually, I'm going to tell you some of the things that you want to include in your videos. I want to talk to you about why you should include these things.

And then, we're going to jump into the how-to stuff, which are things like how to shoot your videos. We're going to talk about how to record audio and how to edit your videos. Finally, we're going to jump into how to upload your videos to get them out to the world.

Anyway, I'm going to jump over to the computer and show you some really cool stuff.

Russell Brunson
Gary Vaynerchuk
Grant Cardone
Billy Gene

"You have an amazing talent and I'm so grateful we met." Russell Brunson

All right, so I've already talked a little bit about who I am, so here's just a couple of my favorite pictures from some of my favorite mentors that I've had the good fortune of meeting over the last couple of years. Russell Brunson, Gary Vaynerchuk, Grant Cardone, Billy Gene, to name a few.

First, let's talk about what we're going to be covering. Number one, what is a video business card. Number two, what should I include in my videos and number three, how to create a video.

One of my favorite quotes is, *"If you own a smartphone, you can create a video,"* and I strongly believe in that. We all have video cameras in our pockets right now.

What is a Video Business Card?

Let's talk about what a video business card is. It's a way for your potential clients or customers to virtually meet you without having to waste their time or yours.

How many times do you get on the phone with somebody and they have a million questions for you about what you do and how you can help them?

A video business card pretty much eliminates this problem. It's a way to gain trust with your potential clients and customers. It's a way for them to learn more about who you are, what you do, where you do it, why they should hire you and how they can work with you and your business before ever picking up the phone.

It's also a really good way to screen people in or out before you ever speak with them or meet with them in person. It's also a huge time saver for yourself and your staff, so you don't have to spend as many hours on the phone or responding to inquiries, answering questions and scheduling appointments with people that never are going to pan out.

What Should Your Video Include?

You want to talk about who you are, introduce yourself, tell them what your name is, talk about your credibility and your experience. Maybe even talk about some accreditations if you have those.

Talk about how many years you've been in business, how long you've been doing what you've been doing, how many people you've helped, and anything else you can think about that would build more credibility into who you are.

Next is what is your area of expertise. What are the benefits of your treatment? How does what you're offering help the individual watching the video?

Next is where are you located? How far is your geographical reach? Who do you serve? Are you mostly online or do you have a brick and mortar location that people would actually physically go to?

Then, why should somebody choose to work with you? What sets you apart from everyone else in the industry? Why should someone trust you?

This is a really good opportunity to include video testimonials from past clients if possible. What you want to do is interview some of your past clients on camera and ask them things like, "What was your experience working with me? What were the results that I got for you? Why did you enjoy working with me? Why did you prefer to work with me versus someone else down the street?"

Video testimonials are the most powerful marketing tool you can use to sell other people on why they should work with you.

Then, lastly, how can somebody get a hold of you? You want to include your website. Maybe your phone number, your physical address, and your email. Maybe not all of those things but a couple of ways that somebody could get a hold of you so they can start working with you.

Now here are a couple of bonus items for you; Share some success stories that you've had over the years. Sometimes you can't get people on camera to do a testimonial video, so this is a great opportunity to share some success stories of results that you've generated for someone.

One of the most important components of the video business card is to cover the frequently asked questions that you find yourself getting asked the most.

What are those frequently asked questions that people are calling in and asking you or emailing you on a daily basis? You want to make sure that you cover these questions in your video.

Providing answers to common questions will dramatically reduce the number of people who are calling in and wasting your time and asking you questions when you can simply cover this on your video, so you don't have to worry about it anymore.

How To Create Your Video

Now, let's talk about the fun stuff. Let's talk about how to create your video. We're going to talk about how to plan, shoot, edit and upload.

Step #1: Plan your script.

Build a script based on what we talked about earlier, the who, what, where, why and how.

You can also use video hacking, and if you don't know what video hacking is, go to kevinanson.com and download my free video hacks cheat sheet. It goes through step by step how you can hack other people's videos.

Basically, you're ethically stealing someone else's format that they use to create their video. What you want to do is go on something like YouTube or Facebook and find another video in your niche and dissect the elements within that video so that way you can figure out how they created it, what their script looked like and then create your own video from that.

The next thing you want to do is you want to either memorize your script or use bullet points.

If you're good at elaborating off of bullet points from a piece of paper, I would highly recommend doing that or if you can memorize your script, do that.

But you're going to want to rehearse it as many times as you can. Rehearse it with someone else. Rehearse it with a family member and have them give you honest feedback because if you sound like you're reading something, your audience or your viewer is not going to believe what you're saying.

This leads me to my next point. Never, ever, ever read from a piece of paper or a teleprompter unless you're experienced to do so.

I can't tell you how many times I've seen people create videos and they make the most amazing script, and then they sit there, and they read it from a piece of paper line by line, and it just sounds robotic. It just sounds terrible because there's no personality. There's no authenticity. It doesn't come off as genuine.

Whatever you do, if you create a script and you're reading it back on camera, make sure to memorize it. Use bullet points or just make sure that you know what you're doing if you are going to be reading it verbatim.

Step #2: Make a shot list.

Now, let me just preface this with not everyone is going to need to make a shot list. I'll give you an example of when you will not need to make one.

If you're shooting yourself talking on camera, it's just you. We see your face the entire time; you probably don't need to make a shot list because we're just going to hear you talking the entire time. That's just one long shot, and that is all.

But if you're creating a video where it's you talking on camera as well as cutting to different shots that supplement what you're saying, you're going to want to make a shot list.

Let me give you an example of that. Let's say you're talking about, I don't know, maybe a coffee cup on the table. You're like, "This coffee cup blah-blah-blah." We see you talking on camera, and then you're going to want to cut to a shot of the coffee cup while you're still talking.

That's an example of what they call B-roll or footage. It's you talking while we see a different shot.

In this case, you're going to want to make a shot list of all the different types of shots that you want to get to tell the story within your video.

Now, this might include shots like the exterior of a building, the interior of a building and you want to make sure you shoot wide shots, medium shots, and close-up shots.

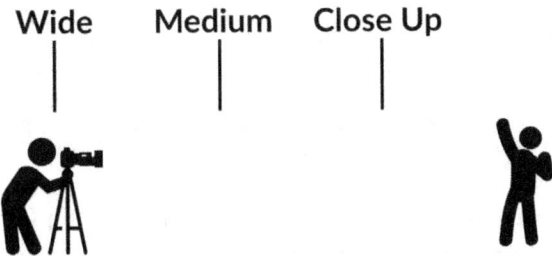

Wide   Medium   Close Up

What I mean by that is let's say you're inside of an office building and you see a bunch of cubicles. Say there are 20 cubicles inside an office.

You get a wide shot. It's where you can see all 20 cubicles in the shot.

Then, you get a medium shot. Maybe the medium shot is just one cubicle. You see somebody working there, a person at a computer.

Then the close-up shot might be maybe just their eyes focusing. They're working, or maybe their fingers are typing on the keyboard. That's an example of a close-up shot.

It's kind of like you're telling a story. You're setting the scene. You show a wide shot, all the cubicles; medium shot, the one cubicle; the close-up shot, it's just the person working on the computer. You see their eyes or their fingers.

That's an example of the sequences that you can be shooting. Make a list of all the different shots that you want to capture for your video and always think of it like wide shot, medium shot, close-up shot.

For every shot sequence that you get, you want to get at least three shots within that environment.

Let me give you one more example. You're at the beach, and we see a wide shot of the beach. Then the medium shot could be you're playing in the sand. Finally, the close-up shot is showing your feet digging in the sand really close up.

That way, it gives the viewer an idea of the surroundings, and that's what B-roll is. That's an industry standard term that is used to refer to footage. When you're capturing additional footage to supplement the narration within the video, it's called B-roll.

Step #3: Basic equipment.

What type of equipment do you need? For this training, all I'm going to talk about right now is using your smartphone.

Of course, there are dozens of different cameras that you can go out and buy. You can get all these great lenses and different attachments and all these fun, cool tricks and things like that.

But for now, all I'm going to tell you guys is if you've never created a video in your life, or maybe if you have and you're afraid of producing a video for your company, all you really need is the smartphone that's in your pocket.

Now, whether you're on an iPhone or an Android, the app that I highly recommend is Filmic Pro. You're going to want to download this app and play with it and the reasons why are; you can set your exposure, which is basically the brightness of your shot and you can set your focal point. To make sure that you are in focus or whatever you're shooting is in focus.

The basic stock camera app that most of these smartphones come with is not the best app to use if you're trying to create a professional video and here's why - You know how when you point it outside, the exposure adjusts accordingly or you point it inside, and the exposure adjusts. It's always adjusting the brightness and contrast while you're shooting.

That doesn't look very professional. That's why Filmic Pro is a great option to make sure that it looks professional for your business.

Now, if you're shooting yourself on camera, and let's say you don't have anyone else to help you shoot it, or you just want it to be a nice steady shot, I would highly recommend getting a tripod. Amazon sells a bunch of different tripods for smartphones. Just do a quick search, and you'll find some really good ones. Just sort by the ones that have the best reviews, and you'll be on your way.

Now, for sound, if you want to shoot with just the microphone that your smartphone has, you'll probably be okay, but if you want to take it up a notch, I would highly recommend getting the SmartLav by RODE.

It's a great microphone that plugs right into your smartphone. A wire connects the mic to your smartphone, and the mic can be attached to your shirt via a clip. You simply talk into the mic, and it just sounds really nice. There's also an app that goes with it so that way you can monitor your sound levels, making it easy for you to produce professional quality audio.

Now, as far as lights go, if you don't want to invest in lights, you don't have to. I would simply recommend shooting during the day. Shoot near a window so that way you can make sure there's sunlight coming in through the window onto the subject's face.

If you do want to get lights, this is a great lighting kit that you can get on Amazon, or if you want to, of course, go into Amazon and search by the ones that have the best reviews.

That's completely up to you, but as I mentioned before, you don't have to get lights. If you're just getting started with creating a video, I would simply recommend using whatever natural light is already in your environment.

Shooting guidelines

Now, as far as shooting guidelines go, one of the most important things that I always tell my students and one of the biggest mistakes that I see when people are shooting a talking head, is they leave way too much room above the person's head. Don't make this mistake.

Another thing that I would recommend is to make sure that there is a lot of depth in your shot. If you're shooting yourself on camera, don't shoot yourself up against the wall. Make sure there are things in the background to see. Make sure your shot has depth. That way, it draws the viewer's eye into you, the one speaking.

Always follow the rule of thirds

If you're doing an interview style shot, make sure you follow the rule of thirds. To do this make sure the person is either framed on the left-hand side or the right-hand side of the frame. I cover a lot of this stuff in my course, to which you'll find a link to at the end of this chapter.

Now here's a bonus tip. This is something that I like to do when I go out shooting for clients. I do what's called a tour. If you guys have a clinic or a practice, give the viewer a tour of your premises where you're actually walking around and showing them the place and talking about it, like do a walk and talk.

You're like, "This is the front entrance. This is the reception area," or go back in the back. "This is where we do our treatments," all the different things that you want to share, do a walk and talk.

Those things are extremely popular, and people love to see the environment before they go and actually do business with you.

Another thing you want to make sure you do on camera is have a ton of energy. I know it's hard and I know it's awkward, but when you're on video, you'll have to have ten times the amount of energy that you would normally have in real life.

For example, as I'm recording this right now, my hands are flailing all over the place, and I'm getting very excited and I'm trying to have a bunch of energy, but I don't talk like this when I talk to my wife or my kids, I have little bit less energy. I'm a little more monotone. You have to have energy when you're on camera. If you want people to believe in what you're selling, if you want people to like you, if you want them to trust you, you've got to have a bunch of energy.

I always tell people, "Give your delivery so much energy that it just feels ridiculous," like it just feels fake. And nine times out of ten, when you watch the video back, it's going to feel right, you're going to watch it and go, "Oh that feels really good to me."

Make sure to have as much energy as you possibly can to the point where it's just uncomfortable. That is what you want to be doing.

Step #4: Post-production

Now, let's talk about step #4 which is post production or compiling your video. This is where you're going to start editing your video together.

Now, if you guys don't want to edit on a computer and you just want to keep it as simple as possible, and you want to edit only on your smartphone, you can do that.

I've edited tons of videos on my smartphone. I've actually shot videos and edited them right from my smartphone. For me, I have an iPhone, so I use iMovie, or I'll use Adobe Premiere Clip.

If you're on an Android phone, I know there's a ton of different video editing apps. You could just Google the best ones. I've heard of apps like Filmora, or ActionDirector. You can also use Adobe Premiere Clip on the Android.

Now, if you want to edit your video on your computer, there is a whole host of different apps that you can use to edit your videos on the computer.

For me, I use Adobe Premiere. That's my favorite editing platform. It does everything that I need it to do. Maybe if you're on the Mac and you just want to keep it simple, you can use iMovie, or you can use Final Cut Pro X. On the PC, the most popular one I hear all the time is Camtasia. There's also Adobe Premiere on the PC as well.

Now, don't be intimated by editing your videos. It's actually much easier than you might think especially if you're just staying on your smartphone.

It might take a little bit of getting used to, just like anything, but once you figure out how to use the app, it actually goes pretty quickly. And especially if you're just doing a very simple talking head video, if you did a good job of scripting out your video and planning out your shots, the editing process shouldn't be all that difficult.

Now, if you want to add music to your videos, my very favorite site in the whole world for getting a royalty free music is audiojungle.net. And my second favorite is premiumbeat.com. There will be a link to a list of resources at the end of this chapter.

As far as voiceovers go, let's say that you want someone to read your entire script and you don't want to go on camera at all. You can do that too.

The guy that I use for my voiceovers all the time, and I'm going to throw his name out there because he's amazing is Alex Rain. You can send him an email, alex@alexrain.com, or just go to his website, alexrain.com. He's an amazing male voiceover artist. I use him the most.

If you want to save some money and budget is a little bit of an issue for you, go to speedyspots.com. They have super affordable voiceovers. They have male and female. They have different dialects, different types of voices that you can choose from, different characters. I love Speedy Spots. I've been using them for probably ten plus years. There's also voices123.com and voices.com.

Step #5: uploading your video

Once you export your video, you're going to want to upload it somewhere so people can see it. The first place that I would upload it to is YouTube and then the second is Facebook.

I would actually do both of these just to make sure you're getting as many views as possible, and if you want to upload it to Vimeo as well, you could always do that.

I use Vimeo for my own business because I think it's a great platform to store all of my videos. It has a lot of great tools that I use for my clients to be able to review their videos, make notes, download their videos, things like that. But I think you'll be fine with YouTube and Facebook because those are both free.

Wistia is another platform if you're worried about somebody stealing your video because they have a lot of security built in the platform. And it's just a great way to host course videos if you're doing that as well.

Useful tools and resources

Let's say you're working on a video where you're not able to capture all of the shots to supplement your video. That's where B-roll comes in, or footage.

There are awesome websites like videohive.net and videoblocks.com. Let me give you an example. Let's say you don't want to be on camera at all, and you don't have anything great to show like maybe your office doesn't look that great, or maybe you only have a home office, but you still want to make a really nice looking video.

What can you do? You write a script and send it out for voiceover. You get a voiceover file back, and then you could actually make the entire video with just B-roll.

While the person is speaking, the voiceover person, you just buy a bunch of B-roll from VideoHive or VideoBlocks, and you can create a video from scratch. You never even have to pull out your camera at all, and you can create a very nice video from essentially nothing.

Now, the prices of B-roll vary from VideoHive to VideoBlocks, but on average, you can buy a great video clip on VideoHive for around $10. VideoBlocks allows you to set up a yearly subscription for between $10 to $15 a month and you get access to a lot of their library, which is super affordable, and they have some really great footage on there.

When it comes to sound effects, there are a lot of free videos on YouTube where people upload sound effects, and you can download those YouTube videos for free.

I use the 4K Video Downloader. Just type that into Google, it's a cool little plugin that you can use. You just paste the YouTube link into the 4K Video Downloader, and it will download the sound effect file into an MP3 right on your computer.

An example of sound effects might be that you want the sound of waves crashing or seagulls, or you want sound effects of a door slamming, glass shattering or any sound you can imagine.

Sound effects are just really nice to have in your video sometimes if you want to enhance the viewing experience and add an extra layer of professionalism.

Audiojungle.net is another place where you can purchase sound effects. They're usually around a couple of dollars, $5 at the most where you can purchase really high-quality sound effects.

As far as music goes, I talked about this earlier. There are audiojungle.net and premiumbeat.com. Just set up an account. The average cost of a song in AudioJungle is around $19. The average cost on PremiumBeat is around $50 to $200 per song.

And then, of course, I talked about voiceovers, so there's my man, Alex, at alexrain.com. Super awesome guy. He does amazing voiceover work. He's very affordable as well. Speedyspots.com, voices123.com, and voices.com.

As far as editing software on your smartphone on the iPhone, there's Adobe Premiere Clip. There's iMovie. There's InShot. The only thing about Adobe Premiere Clip is you have to have an Adobe account to use the software.

On Android, there is also Adobe Premiere Clip. There's ActionDirector. There's FilmoraGo. There's a whole bunch of different editing software that you can get on Android and iPhone.

Just go to the app store and search for the best ones. Look at the reviews of course, but there is just some really great editing software out there these days.

As far as desktop editing software goes, my favorite and I'm on a Mac, is Adobe Premiere. You can also use Adobe Premiere on the PC. On the Mac, there is Final Cut Pro X as well as iMovie.

On the PC, there is Camtasia, Pinnacle, Movie Maker. Number one, of course, Adobe Premiere.

Here is another cool little hack for you. It's called the script time calculator. Just search for it on Google, and you'll find this website by Edge Studio. What it does is you can type in the number of words in your script, and it will tell you how long your video is going to be.

Let's say you're aiming for a 60-second video. You write this great script. Count the number of words that are in your script and then type that number in. It will tell you how long it's going to be. This is a super helpful tool to help make sure you keep your word count within a reasonable range as well as making sure that your video ends up being as long as you want it to be.

All right, guys, and that concludes this presentation. Now, I just want to say for some people; video is going to be very hard at first. Creating a video the first time is going to be awkward. It might not go very well. You might fail a couple of times. You might make a video; you start editing it, you're just not happy with it. Don't give up. Keep creating videos. It's just like anything in your life when you learn to play a sport, baseball, basketball, whatever it is, it's not always easy at first. It takes a little bit of practice.

But you can create awesome looking videos pretty much for free. You don't even need to buy anything. You have your smartphone. You have a number of free apps on the smartphones that are available to you to make videos for free or for very little outlay.

I would highly recommend that you download my cheat sheet at kevinanson.com. It's just a really great cheat sheet that tells you step by step how you can actually hack other people's videos.

There's a lot of videos out there in the world. There are good videos, and there are bad videos.

Of course, you want to find the good videos that have lots of views. I'm sure they're generating a ton of results if they have a lot of views on YouTube or Facebook.

Download my cheat sheet. Read through that and find out the best way to actually hack other people's videos. I have a course. It's called Video Hacks for Entrepreneurs. If you go to bitly/videohackscourse, it will take you straight to the landing page where you can purchase my course.

Inside that course, I go into much more detail about getting started with video. There's a whole 45-minute training module that dives into editing, for example, in Adobe Premiere, how to start bringing your footage in, how to edit it. If you guys are interested in that, check out bitly/videohackscourse.

Then, I have an amazing Facebook group if you go to bitly/videohacksforentrepreneurs. This is just the most incredible community that we've been building over the last twelve months.

Everyone in there is just super passionate about video. There are people from all walks of life. There are people from all skill levels from amateur all the way up to expert.

It's just a great place to go and to share what you're doing. Maybe you want to share a video that you created and get some feedback. I would highly recommend joining that group. It's a free Facebook group. It's a private group, so you have to request access to get in.

Thank you, guys so much for reading this chapter. I really appreciate it. If you guys ever have any questions at all, please feel free to reach out to me. The best place to get me is in the Facebook group, or if you want to add me on the Facebook, or you can try me on Facebook messenger, I just love helping other people get started with video.

I like to help them get started and create awesome content because video is so, so powerful for anyone's business. No matter what you're doing out there, video is the number one tool for growing your business and growing your audience.

Thank you, guys, for reading.

Are you interested in creating videos that grab attention and bring clients to your door? Check out Kevin's latest course at videom8rix.com and of course make sure to join his Facebook group at https://bit.ly/videohacksforentrepreneurs

Enjoying this book so far? We'd love it for you to share your thoughts and post a quick review on Amazon!

Please leave a review at gwpms.com/vsp-review

Work with What You Have and Make Video

Hey, guys. My name is Robert Gardner. I own the business Robert Gardner Wellness, and I cut my teeth as a massage therapist and then later as an educator teaching Thai massage, and now Reboot 21st-century manual therapy.

I'm going to give you a quick synopsis of what happened and a trajectory through my business in dealing with social media and video production.

I wanted to use this video as an example of how I deal with social media production and how I deal with things.

Many people that I talk to are nervous about making videos. They don't feel comfortable on camera. They don't like posting photos online, and what I can tell you is that this is the most potent communication tool that connects to the internet that has ever been developed.

Don't worry about the quality

I don't want you to worry, just like I'm not worried right now about the quality of this video. I didn't have time to get a videographer to put nice frill and logos and stuff.

This is going to be single, raw take. It's going to be warts and all, flubs and all, and that is really what I'm trying to demonstrate to you.

To give people very high-quality content, you do not need an expensive camera. I did build up to this camera that I'm recording with. It's on a tripod. The video has to be a little bit under 30 minutes due to the quality setting I've chosen.

Literally, all I did was set it up and press a button. I've got a light just over here that essentially is just a lamp on a stand with four bulbs and an umbrella that softens the lighting.

I've built up to this point. I have not shaved today. You can't really tell. The video's going to look fine. The audio's going be good. I'm not even wearing a wireless mic.

Here's the thing, for you to really excel online and to produce content, you don't need any of this equipment. You already have what you need to get started. I'm going to talk about how I took my business from my private home studio to begin the process of revolutionizing massage in the United States, in my home country, and then slowly online.

The power of online digital distribution

Years ago, the problem that I had, much like many of you wellness professionals, is what do you do? What is your niche? What do you specialize in? And how do you get people interested and involved?

Alright. In my case, I taught Thai massage. I was doing Thai massage sessions, and I was doing okay getting clients. My practice was growing and thriving, but it got to a point where I knew I was going to be booked out. I wasn't going to have any time to be able to teach classes, and there was going to be a limit to the number of people I could help simply for the fact that, well, I can only work on one person at a time.

I knew that, since my practice was growing, there was a market for what I was doing, and it was generally unavailable.

What I did was I started teaching, and when I started teaching, I got into a very different realm because for the first time, I started to think about, well, people might need a workbook. They might need something to supplement my class to be able to give them a template, a sequence to follow. So I made a very rudimentary copy of what became this workbook.

Now, this is glossy. This is printed. This is spiral bound. These photos were professionally shot. The text was edited by an editor because my grammar isn't so great. This was professional.

When I started, it was just photos of my wife's son. I'd drawn on him with a Sharpie to try to show the sun lines from Thai massage.

Once I made this, I didn't even have a physical copy. What I had was a PDF, a very small, digital file, and my first set of thoughts were this. I was trying to educate people about Thai massage. I was trying to educate people about what I did, and I said, "Okay, I can sell that PDF. I can sell this workbook if I have it printed."

Okay. So now you're thinking retail because retail is going to supplement your practice if you're anything like me.

Then I was making videos to make people aware of Thai massage. What essentially happened was this. We set this up on my website with an email capture, and anyone on earth can download an entirely free copy of this workbook. It's 54 pages, professionally shot and done, no expense was spared, for an email address. What that means is I give it away completely for free, and I have people tell me that was the dumbest thing they had ever heard. And I said, "Watch." Because even I, not having a full inclination, knew when people want something for free, would they give me an email address, and here's what happened.

I went online. I started posting about that workbook. I started posting the free link so people could download it, and within a couple of weeks I had over two thousand downloads, and I went, "Whoa! Wow! Two thousand people."

Here's what happens when you access and harness the power of the internet via video, via digital distribution, whether that be YouTube or on your website, on your blog, having a podcast, whatever it is you're doing to market using this technology. You reach out to a much wider audience.

Now, if you sell an in-person service, and you live in Phoenix, Arizona, you're first thought is you can't sell something to someone in New York, and that is partially true. But if you build a following, it increases internet traffic, it increases social media exposure, and it increases search engine optimization. Okay?

Here's what I chose to do. In addition to having that free workbook, I continued to go ahead and make more content, and the smart thing I did was I made a DVD. I made a video that was, again, available digitally for a small fee, and it was also available as a DVD that people could buy.

The video follows this workbook page by page. So even if you get this for free, you want to buy this. Then, because my love was mat-based work, massage therapists started asking me for table based Thai massage. I wrote a workbook that was three times as long. Still the same high quality, professional, glossy photos, great text. It was 142 pages. I charged for the PDF.

Then we made a second DVD set that goes over that workbook page by page. Again, because if you've got the workbook, you want the DVD because you want to see it. It's movement based, right?

I don't think that online is a perfect way to Thai massage, but I did it. Then I went back to my real love, which is mat-based. I made a 220-page workbook with a completely different sequence with the same great quality photos and text going over more information than any wellness professional could use in their practice. Then came the three DVD set. Same thing follows the other one.

Finally, we got to phase two, which was Sidelying. In Sidelying, this was 262 pages, so we start small, and you funnel them to a larger purchase and a larger workbook and more depth. The DVDs for this should be out in about six weeks.

I have that full retail package that I can now sell to somebody who lives somewhere else. They can live in Phoenix, New York, Australia, New Zealand, Japan, South Korea, they can live anywhere, and they can start studying with me at home. That all started because of this little free PDF.

When you release something online digitally, it does not have to be the highest quality material imaginable. You want it to provide value because it's going to represent your brand, but you don't have to spend as much money as I did.

You can literally make a little two, three page PDF that can provide people great value depending on what part of the wellness professionals industry you are. If you're an acupuncturist, a chiropractor, massage therapist, physiotherapist, there are so many different little niches in our industry, when you provide valuable content, people will respond to that.

Authenticity and transparency build your brand

You start with your phone. You start where you are, and one of the things that comes up for me is transparency, authenticity, ethics, and integrity.

I talk about these regularly in my business because I'm getting massage therapists to trust me as an educator. People will not purchase or buy from people they do not like, admire, and trust.

The way that I build that trust is using video and social media engagement, but what I really want to stress to you is it's not

Hollywood anymore. The technology has de-centralized video production, and anybody can do it.

When you present your true authentic self, act naturally, like when I drink tea on camera it helps build my brand, you're like, wow, Robert's just a normal guy just like me, and I say, "Yes, and just like you, I was a struggling massage therapist who built his practice, and you can, too."

That may be part of your story. What I want you to think about is when it comes to authenticity, when it comes to transparency, ethics, integrity, social media is really good at documenting, not Hollywood, social media is really good at documenting your life and the message that you're regularly telling your potential buyers, consumers, and clients. Whatever that may be within the wellness industry.

Do you need high production value? I don't think so. Here's what I'm going to say for most of you. Maybe you're out there, and you're uncomfortable on camera. That is a totally legitimate thing, and I want you to start small because the video I'm producing here is extemporaneous. This is not scripted except for a little outline. Okay?

If you feel uncomfortable, I want you to think about what an Instagram photo does. A Facebook post, a photo, little text, Twitter, SnapChat, YouTube, a minute video on Instagram, a minute video on YouTube.

If you don't feel comfortable producing long-form content, you can produce short-form content, and you can do it with the equipment you already have. It doesn't cost anything.

I guarantee that you can go online and figure out how to make your own PDF for free. It will probably cost almost nothing to go ahead and do that.

You have the technological capacity to do really great things if you harness the power of this, the most potent communication tool ever developed.

If you make money, and you want to grow, sure, get a videographer, get a higher quality camera, get something that goes past 30 minutes, invest in lighting, invest in a backdrop.

Do I have a backdrop? No. I'm just in my home studio on my couch where my clients come in and sit down before we start a session.

Transparency. It builds a personal brand. It brands me as someone who is authentic and real, and that is something Hollywood hasn't mastered.

They can give a glossy image, but can they give people that are real, that are relatable, that are approachable? That is part of what I build my personal brand on using a fairly inexpensive camera, and, in my case, a smartphone.

This was really where I started. I started with a flip cam that was much less powerful. The video quality and audio quality was much worse than what is on this phone right now. You do not need high production value.

Be funny, interesting and informative

When it comes to social media posts, what do you have that's funny, interesting, informative, and in the end, is worth seeing, much less paying attention to?

When you go to Instagram, I want you to take note of what you pay attention to. Is it funny? Is it sexy? Is it food photos that are nice, make you hungry? What is it that you respond to in social media posts? You have to share content that engages people in your story.

One of the things I do as I'm building my personal brand is my Instagram is also full of food photos. The reason it's full of food photos is it diversifies my content, it makes people want to check out my profile, and hey, when I'm in Austen, Texas having tacos, other people go, hey, I like tacos, and they like my post.

When they like my post, they're more likely to see me in their feed again and again when I'm also referencing that I have a Thai massage session available, when I have a Thai massage class available, when I have retail material for sale, when I have a subscription service for sale.

They're more likely to see those posts as well as the posts where I take pictures of my roommate's dog and show how annoyed the dog is about me booping her nose, booping her nose, booping her nose, booping her nose, booping her nose. Why? Because it helps build a personal brand. Hollywood is dead. It's coming. You need to get on board now and start small, where you're at with your phone.

When we talk about content, again, what's funny, what's interesting, informative, worth saying, what's worth paying attention to. You have to give value.

When I say give value, do you inform someone? Do you educate someone? Do you make them laugh? Do you entertain? You have to do those things to be able to engage people in your story.

Social media platforms

When we talk about platforms, we know Facebook, Instagram, Twitter, YouTube and Snapchat, and I want to talk about each of them briefly.

Facebook

Facebook is, currently, to my knowledge, the largest social media platform. It is the most aggressively used and marketed. You can have a personal page. You can have a business page, and we will talk about Facebook groups a little bit later, but you can share content from your personal page and your business page.

For massage therapists, I regularly get the question, well, do I separate my personal and business page? Here's what I want to tell you. You can have a personal page and heavily filter posts using Facebook settings.

I don't. My personal page and business page are essentially the same thing. Now, I'm talking about my experience. You do not have to do this. I just want to make you aware of the parameters.

What I do is I'll take a business post and share it through my personal page, and I'll take a photo of the tacos I made and share it through my business page because myself and my business as a bodyworker, massage therapist, and educator, are essentially feeding each other.

Students often come in, and they like me personally. Once a month, I'll go to my business page, and I'll invite all these people to like my business page. I just didn't care to have a portal to be able to talk to just my friends on Facebook.

Facebook, if you do not realize, (now I'm sitting closer to the camera looking right at you in the eyes), is business. Social media might as well just be called social marketing.

You are distributing and disseminating ideas. That's very easy to do when people like, know and trust you.

Facebook is a really valuable platform, and most people are already on it. It's the one you're most familiar with. I want you to share those photos, videos, on Facebook, and I want you to upload them directly to Facebook because when you upload them directly to Facebook, they give you more exposure and more views because they have a vested interest in keeping people on their platform.

Instagram

Now, Instagram is owned by Facebook. Instagram's functionality is a little bit more like a ticker tape. It's a little bit more like a floating billboard. Less debate, less dissension.

It's floating through what do people like to see video and audio wise? Photo-wise? What's attractive? What's drawing their attention? What's keeping them engaged? What do they like? Is it food photos? It's a ticker tape, and you can learn how to give people value because you take a photo of the flower you saw on your walk because it's a beautiful flower. Who doesn't want to see a beautiful flower?

You can take your picture of the tacos you had for lunch and hashtag tacos, and we'll talk about hashtags, both for Instagram and Twitter, when we get to Twitter, but Instagram gives you, I believe, 30 hashtags that you can use. Those hashtags function as a search function.

Let's say you are a chiropractor in Australia, and as a chiropractor, you want to draw people in your area in Adelaide, in your area in South Australia, in your area in Tasmania, wherever you may live.

You're going to hashtag your country, city, state, then maybe your town, the area that you're in. You hashtag back pain. You hashtag lumbar spine. You hashtag what people are searching for.

You can go on Instagram and do hashtag research. That hashtag research means that when other people are looking for those hashtags, they can find you and if you have interesting content, they can like and share that content.

Twitter

Twitter is a little bit similar. Instagram has picked up over the years. Twitter just upped their character count to 280 instead of 140. Twitter is a really quick way of reaching out to almost anyone on planet Earth who has another Twitter account.

You can @ someone to get their attention. Let's say I wanted to get Idris Elba as a client, and I would @ Idris Elba, try to speak to Idris Elba, I could potentially direct message someone if I had something of interest or import I wanted to contact them about, but it gives me a chance at a dinner party to rub elbows with someone via Twitter.

A lot of the functionality of Instagram is that Instagram is more like a billboard Twitter. Twitter still has a little bit more text. To me, it's a little bit more interactive, but Instagram seems a little bit more video and photo-based than Twitter, but they're somewhat similar platforms.

We discussed Twitter, and how you could contact people, potentially by direct messaging them. I want you to use that sparingly by the way.

There's some complexity to all these platforms. I can't nearly go into all of it just because of how complex each platform can be and how you can communicate using them, but Instagram and Twitter have similar functionality.

I just find Instagram to be a little bit more for a younger generation, and also to be more visual and auditory than Twitter. Twitter is a good space to maybe find articles and network on a broader scale just because Twitter is an older platform, but Instagram is growing rapidly.

YouTube

Now, we've got YouTube. YouTube is owned by Google and is particularly important because so many aspects of marketing and visibility are based around video production. Video production just like this.

If I wanted to, I could upload this video to YouTube. I could use appropriate keywords. I could use a title like wellness professionals, health professionals, social media tips, whatever somebody is looking for.

How to use social media as a wellness professional. How to use social media as a chiropractor, massage therapist. I'm using those keywords because Google is going to bump me up in search engine optimization if I take this video, after using appropriate keywords and post it on my blog.

Now, when I post this video on Facebook, I want to upload it directly because Facebook wants the content on their channel. My YouTube channel has a function for search engine optimization and to share this as an ongoing link because this is easily archived and searchable.

My YouTube channel has become a vault for video production. In that case, what I'm dealing with is I continue to make video content to answer people's questions to be able to increase my personality.

I try to put out at least a video three times a week or every other day. I just give them a little bit of information from my classes, some marketing information, Thai massage information, little snips and pieces of what I do workings with clients, client care, anything related to Thai massage, reboot, manual therapy, stuff that I think would be of interest, and increasingly, interviews.

Sitting with someone on camera or doing something like a Facebook live, downloading that video, and uploading it to YouTube.

The reason is search engine optimization. YouTube becomes long-term storage. I can pull that video out and share it with someone later, repurposing content to be able to float it through Facebook, Facebook groups, on Twitter, Instagram, other places, to give people snippets of my life that are valuable to them.

Snapchat

Snapchat is a younger person's social media. Snapchat has some features that several years ago were unique to only Snapchat.

Instagram, since Facebook owns it, and you'll see this again and again, Instagram is taking features from Snapchat and integrating them over time.

Face filters, things along those lines, were started on Snapchat, but its functionality means that you have a Snapcode. A Snapcode is a visual QR code, which means that someone on Snapchat, they see your Snapcode on your website, they can literally hold up their phone and press a button, and it will add you as their friend or someone they follow on Snapchat. That's what that weird little yellow code is.

Snapchat is a very audio-visual format. I've used it to communicate with students and clients in an off the cuff way. It increases connectivity and information flow. I will occasionally have a student ask me for content or information about classes, and I will answer questions on Snapchat.

I am video communicating with somebody in Sweden, and I'm in Texas because they had questions about something that related to my subscription service. That's a wonderful, quick way of using social media in a way that other wellness professionals are not. If you embrace this, you can do really potent, really good work.

Now, I don't want you to fixate on any given platform. I think what you're trying to do is important. If you're making content just to draw local clients, it's very different than selling retail essentially worldwide, online in digital form.

Different marketing challenges depending on the area of the wellness community that you work in. You have to think about your long-term goals and what's going to happen.

I would probably recommend you start with Facebook, add YouTube, especially videos for search engine optimization on Google, then start to add balls, which is juggling. We've got Facebook; we've got YouTube, we've got blogging, we've got local business directories.

You're juggling. Then you can add Instagram; then you can add Snapchat, then you can add Twitter.

Long-term, I'm juggling all of those to try to draw information and traffic from all those sources.

Part of the reason I do that is I don't own Facebook, and when Facebook goes the way of the dinosaur, I've still got Snapchat. I've still got Twitter. I've still got Instagram. Make sense? If YouTube goes away, well, I still have my videos on Facebook; I have them other places if that makes sense.

We don't own the platform, so it's good to have your own content to be able to share on multiple platforms.

Take action

Now, we've made all of that content. We've talked about what's funny, what's interesting, what's informative. We're saying much less, paying attention to. We talked about the options that you have as far as social media is concerned. Facebook, Instagram, Snapchat, Twitter, and YouTube. Five different platforms.

If I had to say as an actionable step, first you just make content, and making content for all of those five platforms can vary wildly. Find people on those platforms and follow them.

Find people who are doing interesting business stuff on those platforms and follow them with an eagle eye and see how they use the platform. See how they use it organically to build and emulate pieces of what they are doing.

You're welcome to follow my social media to see how that works even if you follow me on Snapchat, you get to see what am I putting on Snapchat. I'm learning and evolving using these platforms just like you are.

I'm a lot further along than I was seven years ago, but when I started, I was a Luddite. I forced myself to learn how to use this because I really wanted to build a business that sizzled, and I knew that this was growing, and it was taking over and changing how marketing was done.

The first step was you make the content. You interact with people with authenticity, integrity, transparency, and ethics. We'll say that's step two.

Step three was you post on those five different platforms.

The next step is you have to promote that content. Let's say you've made a YouTube video. Now what? You can get some organic traffic through YouTube, especially if it's really great content. Probably, in the beginning, it won't be, but don't worry about it. You're going to make more and more and more videos.

You're documenting your process as you go. You're using the mistakes. You're shooting with the camera you've got, not oh, well, I wish I had a videographer, and I wish I had higher post-production value, and I wish, and I wish, and I wish. You start where you are with this.

So, you've made a video. What's the first step? I think your blog. What that means is on your website there is a blog, and you make an informative article because if you were a chiropractor, and you made an article about lumbar spine pain, and how chiropractic helps, with the link to the latest research. You're going to embed that video with a little bit of text on your blog.

Are people more likely to read three pages of text, or are they more likely to watch a video? So, you can sum it up in a single paragraph. Three or four sentences, and then you can give them more content if they want to keep reading but put the video at the top so they can watch the video.

When they watch the video, here's the other portion. You're not just providing information, you're allowing them to see your face, you're allowing them to connect with you, and you're communicating in an intimate way with potential clients or students. That is increasing and building the intimacy and connection with your target market. Blogging is a very easy way to do that.

Then, you have your business and personal Facebook page. If you take that same MP4, that same video file, you're going to upload that on Facebook. Now you're hosting it on two different platforms, YouTube and Facebook.

Now you're going to share this on your personal page. You may share it on your business page, and finally, you're going to share it in a Facebook group. You have to find Facebook groups that fit in and around your niche and start posting content that's of value to the people in that Facebook group.

For you, you may have to do some research because, again, as a wellness professional, you may meet a slightly different category or audience than I am.

What that means is you're making content. It's got to be of value. It cannot be sales. Buy, buy, buy. How many people want to buy? No.

What you do is you provide value, and then you occasionally say, "Hey, I've got some stuff that I offer." And you continue providing value, and I've got some stuff that I offer.

Well, guess what happens when you continue to provide value? They not only like your posts, but they also start to look forward to them.

They subscribe to your blog. They subscribe to your YouTube channel. They're waiting for the next video to come out because they want more information.

When you prime the audience that way, it's much easier to make a sale, and Facebook groups are a really great way of building community rapport around what you're shooting and getting pretty immediate feedback.

When you post a really bad video, you might get some haters. You might get some people saying less than positive things about the video production quality of your video. Hey, don't you have lights? Don't you have a better, you know? It's like, no, I just started with my phone.

You interact with people nicely. You provide content. Facebook groups are a great way of doing them.

There's also Instagram and Twitter interactions, meaning, let's say you establish yourself as a chiropractic expert on Twitter and someone writes you, direct messages you, and says, "Hey, I live somewhere else, but I need help with my low back pain. Do you have any videos for that?"

Then you basically have public Twitter or Instagram back and forth with someone where you're sharing content that's of value to them and, potentially, of value to other people.

I want you to consider that, as social media grows, I expect this sort of interaction is going to take over. You can reach out to a worldwide audience using social media. Using that to be able to build rapport is a really wonderful thing to do for your business longterm.

Then there's Snapchat interactions, which we already mentioned, which is like you're snapping me or vice-versa. We're communicating back and forth. It gives you a chance to network with people in a digital realm.

To me, that's really what Instagram, Snapchat, and Twitter are specifically. I always think of it as a dinner party. Who do I want to talk to? Who do I want to associate with? Who do I want to give value to figure out where the business is coming from?

I'm trying to find the people who are going to help me make some money and help people with my chosen wellness path.

Beyond that, what about podcasts? Podcasts are growing because they're just digital. People can listen to them in their car. They're easily transportable. They're small files, MP3. It's a really good way of having a show, interviewing people, talking about other wellness professionals.

For instance, if you watch this video, and you say, man, Robert knows a lot about social media. I would love to talk about acupuncture and social media. Robert, could I interview you? Sure. If you interview me for your acupuncture podcast, I get exposure to an entirely new audience, but I'm providing you additional content about Thai massage that you may not know.

We would be able to discuss acupuncture and Thai massage as wellness professionals from two different points, making interesting, very fun content that we can float through the website, through social media, and a variety of other platforms.

Now that we've done that, I think that was at least four steps. There's one last step. One of the things you'll notice that I did not talk about is I did not mention paying for ads once.

Throughout all of my social media production up until about two years ago, I never paid for ads. I built all of this stuff organically on my own by seeing clients, saving money, buying equipment, making YouTube videos, doing free content.

Can you pay? Yes. I would recommend that you start with free stuff first using your phone. I didn't buy an expensive two thousand dollar camera. You need to get comfortable making minute videos before you make 15-minute videos before you start documenting hours of video.

You need to learn to write blog posts before you start writing workbooks and developing curriculum and doing what it is you do to diversify income streams. Start small and then grow.

When you have more money than time, then you can differentiate, figure out what you want to pay for.

Right now, in my opinion, for many things Facebook ads are the best bang for your buck. Most people in your local area are using Facebook. They're on Facebook. If they're interested in chiropractic or acupuncture, whatever wellness niche you may be in, they're probably on Facebook. I would say less so necessarily on Snapchat.

That's where you have to be crafty about how you spend your advertising dollar, how you put it together, and how you package and then pay for advertising on those portals.

What I can tell you is that Facebook is a huge pipeline to most of the people on Earth. Huge, vast. Same as Google. This is what you actively get access to on a daily basis. When you pay, this pipe gets much larger. This is what you actually get. This is what you see in your Facebook feed, and when you pay, this pipe gets much larger, and it costs money to advertise.

If you can build organically and get to the point where you're making money, I would start to experiment with various kinds of ads on Facebook and see what can happen.

It also depends on where your target audience is. If they're on Instagram, if they're on Snapchat, then these might be really great platforms to advertise on.

Where are your people? The people you're trying to reach out to? If you master, to a degree, using those platforms organically, say Facebook, then you can start small paying to get more of the pipeline to push that pipeline out. But I really think it starts organically with the most potent communication tool on Earth.

If you need to reach me, please let me know. All of my retail packages, the workbooks, and DVDs are available, both in digital and paper form, as well as a subscription service that has 80 to 100 hours of instructional video content on Thai massage and Reboot, what I call 21st-century manual therapy.

If you have any questions for me or want to reach out, please do. You can simply type in my name into Google, Robert Gardner. Why? Because I produce tons of social media content that boosts me in search engine rankings.

You can talk to me on Instagram, Twitter, Snapchat, and I guarantee that if you write to me on Snapchat, and you send me a video, I will respond in video. It's an amazing communication tool, and most wellness professionals aren't using it.

Other wellness professionals are not bad at what they do; they're bad at business. And business is increasingly going online through social media, which is really social media marketing, social marketing, social marketing production.

I'll talk to you again soon. If you have any questions for me, feel free to contact me. My website is robertgardnerwellness.com, and I wish you a great day.

Now, all of that was extemporaneous. Little outline so that I could talk to you. Now, do you feel more connected to me? Then I win, and I will see you again soon on all of my social media channels. I'm Robert Gardner, and I thank you guys for reading

If you'd like to learn how to Reboot your practice & make more money, then check out Robert's courses at rgwellness.teachable.com/

How to Dominate the Google Local Search Results... for Free

Hi, I'm Tim Cooper and in this chapter I'm going to be sharing with you the reasons why it is so important for you to optimize your business listing for mobile devices.

You see, this is the way people are mainly going to find you in this day and age. We're in a mobile age. If you're not on the first page of Google, and people can't find you, you're going to be missing out on a lot of business.

The point is, if you're not coming up in Google search and your competitors are, then people are going to go to them and not you.

Let me demonstrate something for you. Let's say for example I've just dropped my car off to be serviced, and I've got an hour or so to kill. I think I might want to get myself a massage.

Now, it's as simple as this. I mean, you don't even have to type things in. Watch this, "Okay Google, search for remedial massage near me."

Look at that. Okay? I just told the phone to find a remedial massage service near me. It's just pulled it straight up.

If you're not in the three-pack, if you're not in the top three results that come up, then chances are you're going to miss out on that client.

From here, I would start calling from the top of the list to the bottom of the list to organize my massage. Can you see how important it is?

Out and about, people are looking for different services, looking for things to do. If you're not coming up in those search results, well as I said, you're leaving a lot of money on the table.

Let's go back to my computer now, and I'll show you what you need to do to appear in the results on the first page of Google. What's good about this is it just takes a bit of time, and it's totally free.

To go back over what I was demonstrating as I was walking down the street, say somebody is driving in their car, obviously they can't start typing search requests into their phone, so they're going to use some voice recognition probably. Or maybe they're walking down the street, and their hands are full, but they want to search for something. Well, all they need to do is to activate their search, whether they're on an iPhone or a Google device and speak like this. "Okay Google, search for remedial massage near me."

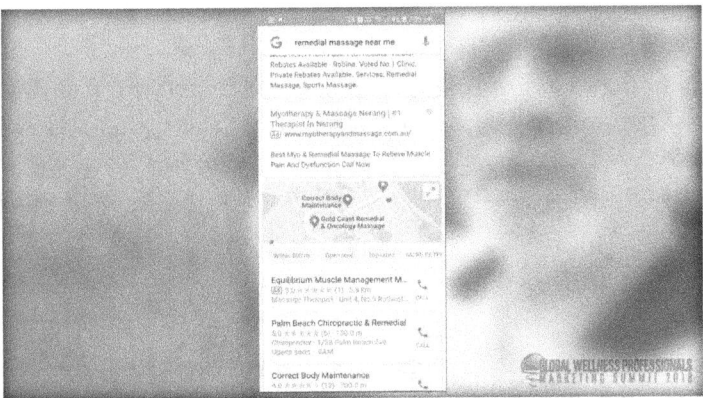

There we have it. Now, why Google? Because when it comes to actually getting clients through your door, people go to Google when they are ready to buy.

That's the difference between Google and Facebook. I'm not saying don't do Facebook, but what you've got to understand is that people don't go on Facebook looking for a solution to their problem. They might stumble across a solution to a problem when they're going through their newsfeed. Something might come up, and they go, "Oh, that's interesting. I'll go look into that."

But people don't go on Facebook to find answers to their problems. People go on to Facebook to socialize, to interact, to see what their friends and family are doing. When we do our Facebook ads, it's what we call interruptive marketing. We're actually interrupting them. We're taking them away from what they are doing.

People may go on Facebook for a recommendation. If, say, they're looking for a massage therapist they may go onto Facebook and ask their friends, "Can you recommend a good massage therapist for me?" But they're not going onto Facebook specifically looking for a massage therapist.

You think about it, what are you going to do if you wake up in the morning and you've got really bad lower back pain, and you don't know a good therapist in your area. You might be traveling, you might be in another city, so you can't see your regular therapist.

What are you going to do?

Are you going to get onto Facebook and put it out there saying, "Can anybody recommend a good massage therapist in this area? Or, are you going to get onto Google and search for a remedial massage therapist near you, and then go through the process of checking their star ratings, reading about them, and picking out somebody who you like?

Nine times out of ten it's going to be the second one, isn't it? Nine times out of ten, when somebody is ready to get fixed, they've got a problem, and they're looking for a solution, they're going to go to Google looking for that solution.

This is what makes getting listed on Google so powerful because you are now reaching the people when they are looking for a solution. When they are ready to act, ready to buy, ready to choose.

The problem with Facebook ads, business cards and fliers is that when you're getting that information in front of your prospects, they may not need you there and then. Yes, they may suffer from lower back pain, but they may not have lower back pain now.

In two weeks, a month, three months, six months down the track when they actually do have a problem, are they going to remember that Facebook ad, that business card, or that flier? Or, in their pain, are they just going to jump on to Google and go, "Get me to a massage therapist quick, where's the nearest one?"

I know what I'd be doing. Can you see the importance? This is why it's so important to get your Google listing created and optimized.

Funnily enough, this is something that a lot of people don't do. They either think it's too hard, they think it's going to be too technical, that they're going to have to get an expert, or it's going to cost too much money, or if they do decide to do something, they don't do it well.

They don't follow the strategy, the blueprint. They don't tick all the boxes. They only do half of it. They miss things out because they don't see it as being important.

This even happens with my own students. I've created a course on local search marketing. When some students contact me and say, "Tim, I'm still not in the three pack." I'll just go through the checklist, "Have you done this? Have you done this? Have you done this?" Or they'll come and say, "Well, I've done this, but I haven't done this, this, and this yet." All I can say in response is, "Well, go and do that, that, and that because you're not going to increase in the rankings until you've done everything."

This is a formula, okay? It's a very simple formula. You don't have to go out spending hundreds or thousands of dollars getting a marketing guru or an expert to do this for you.

This is something you can do by yourself if you're willing to take a couple of hours and go through some very easy to follow steps. But be methodical and have a plan and you can get yourself ranked on the first page of Google for free.

That's another amazing thing about Google is here is your chance to get on the first page of Google, the very first page, up top for free. Other businesses are paying a lot of money per click. They're paying a lot of money per month to list high on that first page.

Yes, Google sees the value in local business. They are making it so much easier for you to get seen on the first page. And, as I said, it's free.

You take a couple of hours to set it up and then spend a few minutes here and there throughout the month each month to maintain it, creating posts, adding photos and videos and getting reviews. I'll talk about that a little bit more later.

The point is there is no ongoing cost involved. Your Google business listing is free, and you will remain high in listings as long as you maintain your listing, as long as you just do a couple of things every month to keep your listing current.

What is the three pack? The three pack is this list of businesses underneath the map.

I'll just go through this quickly on my mobile so that you can see what it looks like in a mobile situation, and then I'll come back on my main desktop machine.

When you perform a Google search on your mobile device the first three or so listings will more than likely be ads. Google places a little green box with the word 'ad' in it next to paid ads to distinguish them from organic listings.

People are paying to be listed here. I can guarantee you the person seen at the very top of this list is paying a lot of money every month to stay there. As you scroll down, the first listing underneath the paid ads is the three pack.

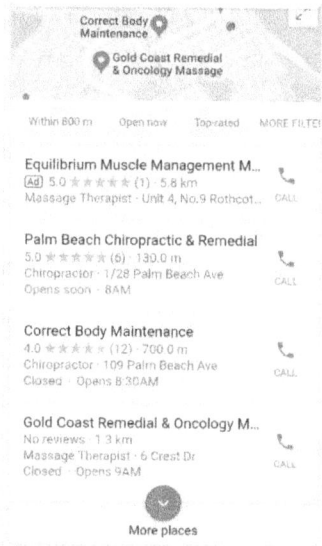

This is the map, and it displays the three best-ranked listings for that area. Now sometimes, this is something that has been available since early 2017, Google now allows you to put a paid ad into the three pack, so it becomes a four pack.

You can see that first listing in the example above; the Equilibrium Muscle Management Massage has got a little green ad box next to it. That means that that's a paid ad.

The next three are organic listings. Those are the listings that are appearing on their own merit, based on their own weight, based on their ranking, okay? That's free. That's what I'm going to talk about in this chapter, how to get into this three pack.

You think about it. You're searching for a solution to a problem, and you bring up that Google page, how far down that page are you going to go to find somebody to ring? Are you ever going to go to the second page?

At the bottom of the three pack, there is a more places button. We can click on the arrow, and it will show us more listings for that area.

But seriously, are you going to go to that second page? Or are you going to go to 'list more places' every time?

Odds are, you're going to start at the top of the list, whether it be that paid ad or the free ones, and you're going to start calling. The only reason why you're going to go onto the next listing is if the first one you call or the previous one you called doesn't suit your needs. They may not have a place for you; they may not have a time that's suitable, they may not have a therapist that's suitable, et cetera.

Generally speaking, that's the only time you're going to go further down that list, isn't it? You're going to keep on going down that list until you hit somebody who can actually help you.

It's usually going to be in those first four or five listings. Generally speaking, it's always going to be on the first page. If you're on the second page of anything, your chances of being seen are very, very low.

That's what it looks like on a mobile device. Let's switch over now to the desktop.

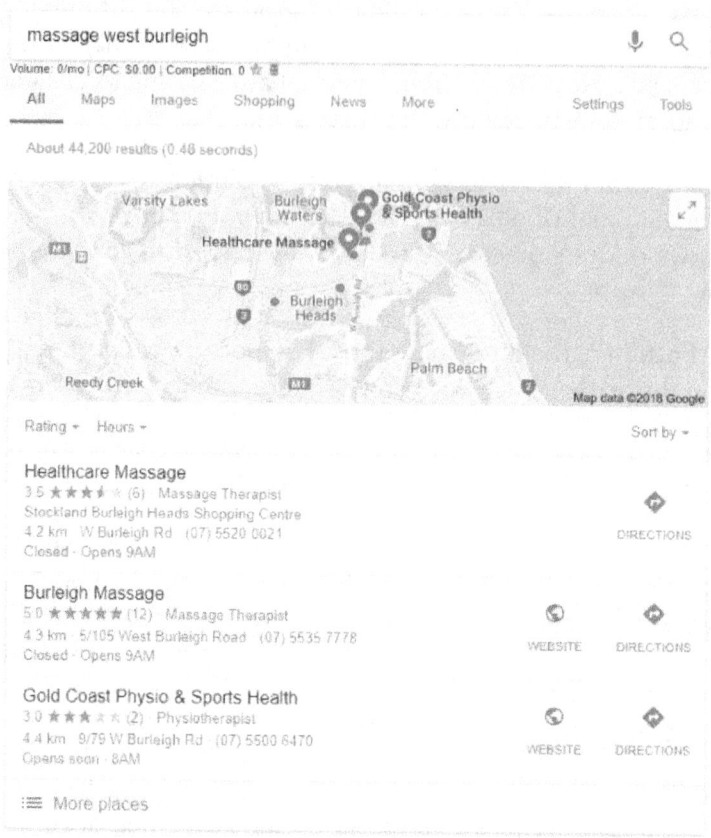

Okay. This is what it looks like on a desktop computer. Of course, this can change. In this example, there are no businesses paying for ads in this area. In massage, West Burleigh, nobody is actually paying to be listed.

The very first listing for this search is the map and the three pack. There are no paid ads being displayed for this search. Now look the good thing about paid ads, and we'll get into this a little bit later in this chapter is that you can now promote to a broader area, to an area that is bigger than your suburb.

The way the Google local listing works or the way the Google business listing works is that it ties you to a suburb when you put in your address, that's your brick and mortar address.

This is for clinics with a physical address, physical clinics, not so much for mobile massage. Although, that being said, once again, Google has recognized the importance of being relevant. They've changed their Google business listing to also allow for people who do service a larger area via mobile massage or whatever industry they're in.

Google is evolving very, very quickly when it comes to what it's offering local businesses, what it's offering you as far as free listings, some free airtime that's worth thousands of dollar to you when you do this right. Once again, it's easy to do this right.

If we go back to the first example I showed you where we had that paid ad sitting in the three pack; you'll see that that actual business is a long way away. It's six kilometers away versus all the other ones around me that are within walking distance. 130 meters, 700 meters, a kilometer away.

The top one is further away. It's letting people reach outside of their suburb, their physical location.

I know it's getting a little bit gray and fuzzy, and maybe a little bit overwhelming, and you might feel like your head is going to explode.

I'm trying to give you a lot of information; I'm trying to give you an overview so that you can see how powerful this is. As I've said, this is so powerful because people go to Google when they're ready to solve their problem. They're ready to get their credit card out of their back pocket. They're ready to book with you. They're serious, okay?

For me, for my time, I would much sooner get my Google business listing set up and working and humming along really well before I would even worry about running any Facebook ads.

You've got to understand that when you're setting up your business or when you're struggling to find clients you've got more time than money.

You've got the time to spend to set up your listing properly. It's not going to cost you any money, but it's going to make you money.

When it came to my business, when it came to attracting new clients to my businesses, I wanted to keep that cost as low as possible. I much prefer a free lead from Google than paying; $3, $4, $5 for a lead through a Facebook ad.

Any honest marketer will tell you that far more campaigns fail than succeed. Any honest marketer will tell you that there is a lot of testing, and tweaking, and fine-tuning involved in getting a Facebook ad that really works and actually generates a lot of money. Before they get to that, they're actually losing money.

They're running tests; they see what works, what doesn't work. When they finally get this formula right, when they finally tweak it and fine-tune it to a point where it's actually performing and performing really well then they turn off all the nonperforming ads and scale up the ads that are working.

They throw a lot of money at it before they find the ad that ticks all the boxes and generates a lot of money before they make their losses back and start to make a profit.

The point is, they just didn't run one ad, and it was a hit, and it made a lot of money for them. It doesn't happen like that in most cases. You might get lucky, but it just doesn't happen like that.

There is no sure thing when it comes to a Facebook ad, and you're spending money. As I said, when you're starting out or when you're struggling, when things are quiet, you've got more time than money, why not spend a little bit of time on setting up your Google listing properly?

Coming back to what I said earlier, a lot of people don't do Google because they don't understand it. They think it's too technical. They think they've got to spend a lot of money, or they don't do it well.

Because of this, in a lot of instances, you can get in the three pack just by doing the basics well. Just by setting that really strong foundation, you can end up in the three pack.

You've got to do all the basics well, all the foundations. This is not a pick and choose situation. You've got to follow these steps. If you follow the steps, then there is a good chance you'll rank high in the search results.

If you're in a highly competitive area, you may have to do a couple of extra things just to get you over the line. But as I said, even today, in this day and age, people still aren't doing Google local search well.

What does it take to do Google local search well? What does it take to come up in that three pack?

Firstly, it takes a complete Google business listing, complete with photos, your business address, your business hours, your phone number. That's a minimum. Make sure all information is complete.

However, simply setting up your Google business listing is not enough to push you up to that three pack, okay? You've got to do more. There are three main things that Google uses to rate and rank your site.

Distance

There is not a lot that you can do about your physical location. If you've got a brick and mortar clinic, there is not a lot you can do about the distance your prospective client is away from your business when they perform their search. But it's important to realize that once again, this is why you should be on Google.

This is why you should have your listing set up nice and strong. As I said, somebody can be walking down the street, pick up their phone and just go, "Remedial massage," or "massage," or "relaxation massage."

Whatever service you provide, they can just pick up their phone and go, "Massage near me." Google using the GPS from the phone and knowing the coordinates of your particular clinic, it's going to show them the clinic that is closest to them first.

This is also why your position in the three pack, even if you're listing is strongly weighted; you can actually slide from position one to two to three and back and forth.

You're in that three pack, but the reason why you slip and slide is that of your location compared to where your prospective client is.

That's one factor that Google uses. Distance from your clinic. Distance from your physical location.

Relevance

The next thing that Google uses is something called relevance. Google doesn't want to display a list of dentists in New York if you're searching for massage therapists in Sydney. Your listing has to be relevant.

In your business title, in the categories that you choose, you've got to make sure that your information is relevant.

Citations

Another thing that Google regardless highly are citations and mentions.

The way to really build up your business listing is to create listings on business directories, good quality business directories. Here while the number of directories you're listing in is important, the quality of the directories you're listed on will determine how much weight Google gives your listing.

For example, setting up your business listings on 20 or 25 good, high-quality business directories is going to be far more beneficial to you than setting up your business listing on 50 low-quality raggy type directories. You've got to pick your directories.

At a minimum, you need to create a business listing on Apple Maps, Bing, Yelp, Yellowpages, and obviously on Google. I would say create your Google business listing first.

Consistency is key

Here is the key, you've got to keep three things consistent throughout all your listings. If you even deviate slightly on any of these details, Google will consider it to be a different business. It won't tally up; it won't sum up everything into one big ranking. You'll be diluting your listings. You'll be confusing Google.

Google won't understand that "drv" is the same as "drive". It's as silly as that sometimes. I'm serious.

The first thing you want to do is to set up your Google business listing. It will give you the address, even if you type the address in one way, it may reformat your address to what matches its database.

Whatever address is listed in Google, that is what you use everywhere. When I was setting up the Google business listing for Massage Schools of Queensland, Google kept reformatting the address to "Level 1/36 Kortum Drive, Burleigh Heads", even though I tried on numerous occasions to enter it as "Level 1, 36 Kortum Drive". Google would not let me do it. Google kept on reformatting back to 1/36.

I had to go back through all the other work that I had done in setting up the school in various business directories and change the address in all those other listings to Level 1/36 so that it matched Google. It was a real hassle and was extremely time-consuming.

I have since set the school up on a subscription service that ensures that the business name, address and phone number is consistent across all directory listings

Three things that must stay the same, identical throughout all your listings is your business name, your address, and your phone number.

I would recommend you set up a text file or store this information somewhere and just copy and paste so that there is no chance of a typo, and that you are guaranteed that your phone number is formatted the same in every listing. Your address is formatted the same in every listing, and your name appears correctly.

If you do this, then this is where you're going to start to build a very strong presence. Google is going to go, "Wow, this business is listed all over the place. It must be good. It must be real. Let's boost it up."

When you're listing in the big, top quality business directories, in the big search engines like Bing, Yelp, and Yellowpages, Google puts a lot of weight on these listings; it scores your business listing higher and the higher you appear in the Google local search results.

Outside of that, where do you put your listings? Every country is different. Every business category is different as far as good listings.

As far as your directories are concerned, you have those main four or five including Google, and then you want to go into high-quality trade listings, association listings, natural health listings, etc. I'm guessing as this is a wellness summit, adding your business to natural health listings would be beneficial.

What you can do if you're not sure which directories you should be listing with is simply search Google for the top directories for your country.

For example, if you were in the UK, you could enter something like, "Best business directories in the UK" and Google is going to return a list of business directories that are highly rated in the UK. Yelp, Yell, thomsonlocal are just a few of the top UK business directories.

In Australia, we've got something called Natural Therapies Pages, which is probably the biggest natural therapies business directory in the country. Obviously we'd be listing with that if we were in Australia.

I'm sure you've got something similar wherever you are in the world as well. You want to list in as many of these good quality listings as possible. Don't just go into one or two. Don't skip Yelp, and don't skip Yellowpages. This is important okay? I've seen this. I've seen people skip these big directories and then wonder why their listing still isn't ranking.

This is why. You've got to list with a lot of these directories and make sure your information is consistent. That's another one. This is a big one. This is something you've got a lot of control over. That's one thing you've got a lot of control over are your listings.

You can't control distance, the distance your potential client is from you. You can't control that. You can control this, you can control the quality of listings and how many you've got, and you can control the completeness of your Google business listing.

Reputation

Now, the other thing that Google takes into consideration is reputation, online reputation. Reviews, right?

Sites like Google, Amazon, and Udemy, put a lot of weight and a lot of value in what others say about you. So do other people. That's why they put a lot of weight in it.

We can tell people we're the greatest service on the face of the earth and we're wonderful, and we can do this and do that. People go, "Yeah, yeah fine."

If somebody else says how great we are, if someone else says what great results we get, then, of course, that carries so much more weight.

It's the same with Google. This is what you do on the maintenance side of things. You start to reach out to your clients and ask them to leave you a Google review. The more Google reviews you get, the better you are going to rank, the stronger you are going to look. Obviously you want good quality reviews, you know, four or five stars.

Here's just a little golden nugget for you. Don't use any of those services that pre-populate the stars.

There are some services that you can use where they give you a short link to your Google review page, and it automatically pops in five stars. Google doesn't like that. If they catch it, they will actually delete all of your reviews.

There are some rules to follow, Google does have an algorithm to work out whether a review is legitimate, or whether it's spammy. Once again, it's an algorithm; it's a machine. Sometimes legitimate reviews are disallowed. I've had that experience in the past. There's not a lot you can do about it. Don't waste time or energy crying over spilled milk. You just have to keep on requesting more reviews.

You've got to ask a lot of people for reviews to get a handful of reviews. It's a numbers game. Even the people who promise to leave you a review often don't.

They say they will, and they mean well, I'm sure they actually do intend to, but when they get to that review page, they may not know what to say, or they feel it's all going to be a bit time consuming or it's a bit fiddly, and they just leave it.

Don't despair. If you ask 100 people for reviews, and you only get 10 or 12 reviews, that's good. 10 or 12 reviews isn't bad for Google. You want to get your reviews to 30, 40, 50, even higher but you know, you just need to get some reviews happening.

Those are things you've got to take into consideration when you are getting your business listing set up to be ranked in Google.

Complete your business listing

Another mistake a lot of businesses make is they fail to complete all the information for their listing.

Here is your chance to climb to the top of the Google local search results for free so take the time to enter all relevant information about your business.

To help Google work out how to categorize your business, you can select multiple business categories. Take the time to review the list and select all categories related to your business. If you can't find an exact match pick one that matches your service the best.

Here's a tip. Different people use different search phrases to find the same service. Think outside the box. What are some categories that are related to your service that people might type into search engines?

Now it goes without saying that you want to ensure your business address is entered correctly along with your business hours.

The 'Special days' field allows you to enter dates that your business is closed. You may close on Christmas Day, New Years Day and other holidays. Simply enter the dates you won't be opening for business. Google then looks at your business hours and displays the days and times you're open except the dates entered in Special days.

You should also enter your phone number and website address if you have one. Photos and videos are extremely important, and you should upload as many photos relating to your business location, services, and staff as you can.

You can create and upload short videos that demonstrate or promote your products and services. Video is only going to get bigger as more and more sites and search engines incorporate it into their platform. There truly is no better time to embrace video in your business.

You should upload some photos showing the outside of your building, parking availability, and the entrance to your business, this way people can see, "Okay, we're driving down the road, oh this is the building here because this is the sign. This is the front door."

Photos of staff, the reception area, treatment rooms etcetera are important as it helps build a sense of familiarity with the prospective client.

Now, I want to show you some insights here. Now, here is proof of just how important having a Google listing is.

Out of 3,859 customers, or prospects who actually searched for the college or related services in one month, 17.5%, 677 people actually searched for the college by name. They specifically typed the college's business name into Google. 17.5% searched by name, which means that 82.5% of people found the college through Google local search results, found the college through searching for either student massage or massage courses, et cetera. Can you see how huge that is?

This is how you broaden your reach. This is how you scale. This costs nothing. Okay? We're getting all this exposure and it's costing nothing.

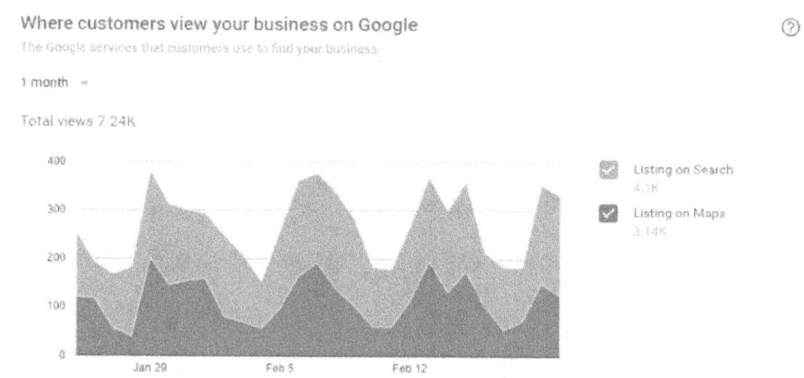

This shows where the college has appeared either in the listings or on Google Maps.

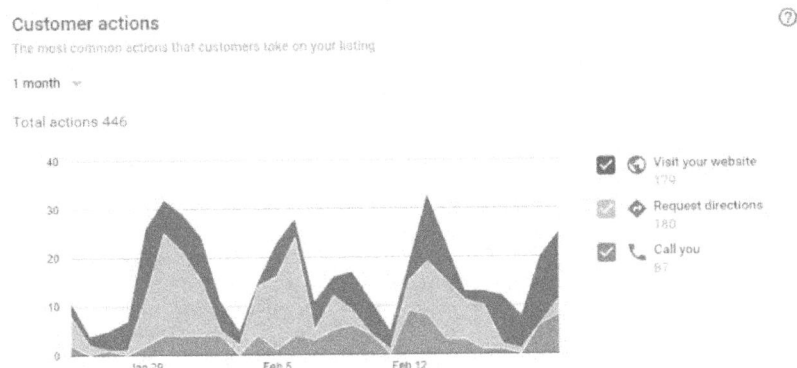

Customer actions
The most common actions that customers take on your listing

1 month

Total actions 446

Visit your website 179
Request directions 180
Call you 87

This is the action people have taken. From this free listing, 179 went onto the website to check out more information. 180 requested directions. How many times has a person been late or no-showed because they forgot where you were?

This is another beauty of Google and Google Maps, if they get lost, they can actually go on, find your business very quickly, and get directions to you.

And here's the really cool part, 87 people picked up the phone and called the college. While the college operates a student massage clinic it's main business is education with course offerings ranging from $350 for a short course to $16,000 for a full diploma. I know for a fact that a percentage of those 87 rang up to inquire about courses, and a percentage of those actually enrolled. This brings in thousands of dollars, and it costs nothing.

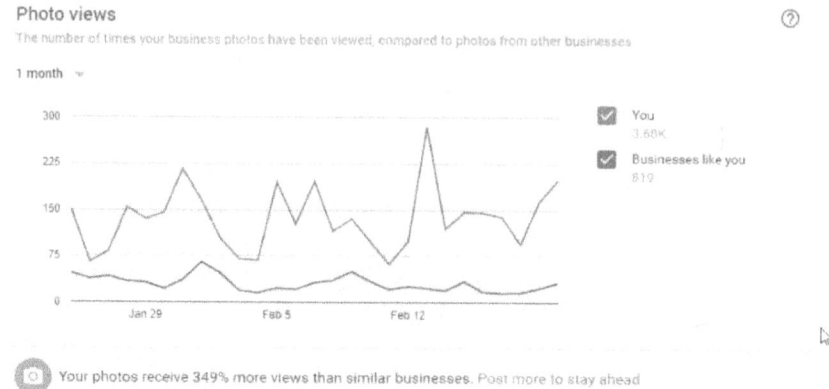

This graph shows how the college's photos are performing. You can see how the blue line is the college and the red line is similar businesses.

You can see how the college is outperforming those businesses with photo views because the college has uploaded a good number of photos. Similar businesses to the college only had on average eight photos while the college had thirteen photos uploaded at the time of preparing this material.

Can you see the importance of uploading good quality images? The images are important in your Google listing. Your outside images help people find you, and the reception images let them know they're in the right place. The point is, it's familiar to them. It feels like they've been there before. It's not a scary experience the first time out because it's comfortable for them. They know where they are, they know what they're doing. Very important.

Let's talk about websites. Do you need a website to be listed on the first page of Google, in Google local search? The short answer is, no you don't.

I have successfully put massage therapists on the first page of Google without a website.

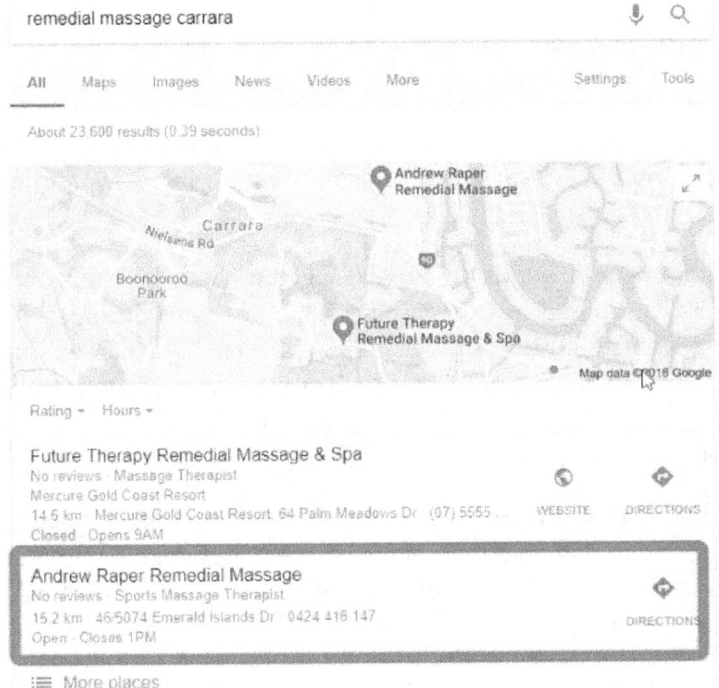

Andrew Raper is a friend of mine, and I set his Google business listing up for him a little while ago. His listing fluctuates between first and second spot. Now, he doesn't have a website. He has nothing. At the time I set this up for him, he didn't even have a Facebook business page. He had nothing. He was totally technophobic. Now he is on the front page of Google for free.

I know for a fact that his business has improved markedly from this listing because he called me not so long ago wanting to take me out for beers and a meal because he's got so many new clients from this listing, so many new repeat clients. It's added thousands to his bottom line every year.

Now, as I said, Andrew Raper had close to no internet presence before we sat down to do this for him. As part of the course I put together for the local search marketing, I actually use Andrew Raper as one of the case studies.

We recorded the whole thing. It's over the shoulder from start to finish. From nothing to being on the first page of Google. From zero to hero. All recorded over the shoulder as part of the course.

As you can see, the answer is no; you don't need to have a website to be listed on the first page of Google, if you're in a low competition area.

The point is with websites is yes, websites can be great for your business, but a bad website can actually hurt your business. A slow-loading website, a sluggish website, a website that isn't laid out well, that isn't designed properly. James Crook did a great presentation on website design for this summit. I highly recommend you go and watch that presentation as well.

The point is that a badly designed website can actually do you more harm than good. You don't need to have a website to get listed, but it's something that once again, you may need to do a little further down the track.

You don't need a website to get started. However, if you're in a high competition area, so say you do all the basics, and you're just outside that three pack, you may be sitting at four or five, then you will have to start to do some extra things to get you over the line.

Google has sort of married organic search with local search. We know for a fact that a well-ranking website is going to boost your local ranking. That's one thing that may help you over the line.

Another thing we've found that has really helped boost our exposure and get the phone ringing are posts.

A Google post appears in what we call the Knowledge Panel. The Knowledge Panel is this box that comes up when somebody searches for you, so for Massage Schools of Queensland, this is the Knowledge Panel that comes up with some photos and information about the school.

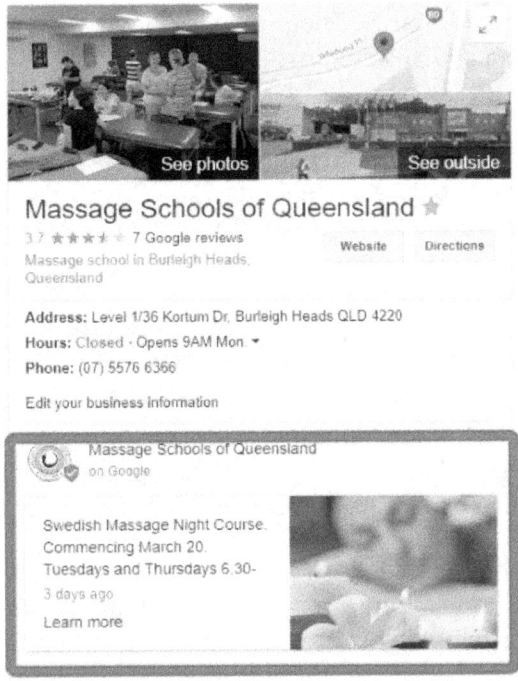

The section where it's advertising Swedish Massage Night Course is what we call a post. Google posts don't last forever. Google posts have got a lifetime of seven days unless you change that. From the time you post your post, it's live for seven days, which is great because it gets you into the habit of posting fresh content all the time. That's one thing that Google loves. We know that Google loves fresh content. I suppose they're enforcing that.

They make your posts go dark after seven days. There's nothing you can do about that. You can start and stop your posts on certain dates. You can schedule them if you've got an event or a promotion, you can schedule your post to go live at a certain day and time, and finish at a certain day and time, you can do that. Generally speaking, your posts go up, and they're live for seven days.

What's been our experience with doing posts? We know that our reach has gone beyond Burleigh Heads. We know we're coming up in search results for a broader area. The phone is ringing with inquiries about the services and courses our posts are advertising.

It's been paying off. The college has been getting a lot of inquiries, and enrollments more importantly, into those courses. Once again, these courses are priced between $350 and $16,000. It's real money. There is real benefit.

The other thing that has been said about posts is that if you do operate a mobile business, by incorporating other suburbs or areas that you service in the text of your post, you come up in those searches as well. You can expand your search area. If somebody is searching massage or remedial massage in the next suburb or a couple of suburbs away and you've included that in the keywords of your posts, then that's another way that you can expand your reach without paying for that ad.

To finish off this section, I want to touch on websites again. Now I haven't spent much time looking at this feature, but Google has created a website builder inside your Google business listing page.

Some people say it's quite good, and it's inside of Google, so it's obviously going to rank and it's going to be indexed by Google very quickly. From what I've seen it builds your homepage automatically based on the business information you provide and the posts you create.

I'll do a separate video training on the Google business listing website builder at another time and put it up onto my free YouTube channel for anybody to watch.

We'll have a bit of a play with it, a bit of an experiment with it, and see how it all comes together. What I would imagine, and from what I've heard from industry leaders is that it's a good concept. It's something that you may look at as well if you don't already have a website and you're looking for something simple, like a placeholder website until you get something more established built.

It's action time

Okay. That's it for this section. The action steps I want you to do is first see what happens when somebody searches for your service offering in your area.

You've got to do this in an incognito window. If you're on Google Chrome, go to your little drop down menu and open a new incognito window. If you're on Firefox, I believe it's called a private window, a private browsing window.

You need to do this in an incognito or private browsing window because Google stores information about what you search for and what you're interested in and if you just search for what you do in your area, the results that come up in a standard browser may not reflect what everybody else is seeing. The results that come up in the standard browser will be modified to suit what you've been searching for recently.

Open up an incognito window or a private browsing window and search for remedial massage New York or whatever you do, wherever you are. Search for that. See where you're coming up. Are you coming up in the three pack? Are you coming up on the first page of Google?

If you're not, then I would urge you to set up your Google business listing. Have you already got a Google business listing? If you have, go in and complete it. Make sure that you've got all the information, make sure that all information is correct. Make it complete. Add lots of photos, inside, outside, showing your work, showing the reception area, showing your clinic room, showing everything.

Then, how many business directories are you listed with? Have you got business listings with Apple Maps, Bing, Yelp, Yellowpages, and the major business directories and trade directories in your area, in your country, in your state?

Once you're all set up, once you've got your business listing all setup, start approaching people and asking them for reviews. Clients that you know are happy with your service, clients you have a good relationship with. Ask them to review your business. Tell them how important reviews are for your business because they help other people find you and make up their mind to come and see you.

There is a way to get a link to give to people that takes them straight to the Google review page for your business so they can just give you a star rating and type in their review.

Those are the steps that I want you to do. It's going to take a little while. If you haven't already got a Google business listing, it's going to take a few days because they're going to send you a postcard. They're going to have some way to verify that you are at the location where you're at because they don't want a lot of bogus businesses on their search. They want to keep their search engines relevant and real.

While you're waiting for your postcard to arrive, take the time to start setting up all the other listings. When you validate your listing, you should find yourself pretty high in the rankings because you've done all this other work.

Then, of course, go forward and keep on doing posts, asking for reviews, and adding more directory listings.

Okay, that's it. Now, I do have a course on this. It is simple. You can do it. Anybody can do it. I've got a lot of successful students from different industries around the world.

You don't have to pay somebody hundreds or thousands of dollars to do this for you. You can do it yourself if you follow the formula as I walk you through it in the Local Search Marketing Secrets course.

In this self-paced, home study course, I lay out the formula for you in simple, easy to follow steps. Then, of course, we've got case studies. We've got additional steps you can take to fine tune, and we've got bonuses on content marketing, video marketing, all sorts of stuff. Great stuff, great course.

As a special offer and thank you for ready this, I invite you to click the link below and take up a very special offer that I've got just for readers of the summit success series. You'll get a major discount on this course.

I'm telling you, just do that calculation here on how much a client is actually worth to you, a happy client. Not a one and done. A client who is actually a repeat client. How much is that client worth to you a year?

How much are their referrals and recommendations worth to you? In a lot of cases, you don't just see the client; the client gets you to see their partner, or their child, or their friend, or their parent. They refer other people to you. Then they become regular.

All of a sudden, regardless of how much you charge per hour, let's work on round figures here. Let's say you charge $100 an hour, and you turn that client into a monthly regular. Well, that one client is worth $1,200 a year.

What happens if he refers his wife and she becomes a regular? That's now $2,000 or over $2,000 a year from one client.

A client who originally found you through Google. It didn't cost you a cent. Because you came up in Google, they came to you. They didn't go to your competitors.

You see the point is, if you don't do this, if you don't get yourself listed on Google, if you don't get yourself listed high in those search results, and your competitors are; you're basically handing business to your competitors. You're making it easy for them. You're taking the competition away from them, okay? They do the work. They get listed. They get the calls.

Now I want you to get those calls. I want you to get listed. As I said, it's easy to do, and generally, people don't do it well. There is a good chance that if you do everything right, you will hit that three pack. I can't guarantee anything, but as I said, I've seen it over, and over, and over again. I know how much it adds to the bottom line, thousands and thousands of dollars, right? At no risk. No risk. People are searching on Google when they are ready to buy. People are searching on Google when they are ready to take action.

You want to be there. I hope you enjoyed this chapter, and I'm looking forward to seeing you on the first page of Google.

EXCLUSIVE SUMMIT SPECIAL: Get Tim's Latest Course '**Local Search Marketing Secrets**' for only $127 **that's a saving of $370!**

localsearchmarketingsecrets.com/summit-special

Want to connect with Tim? Check out his website at

WellnessBusinessBreakthrough.com

Tim also publishes as lot free content on his YouTube channel (https://www.youtube.com/c/wellnessbusinessbreakthrough) and Facebook group (gwpms.com/wbbfacebookgroup).

You can also email Tim at tim@gwpms.com

Building Your Foundation for Awesome Facebook Ads

Hello and welcome to my presentation on Facebook Ads 101. This is all about building your foundation for awesome Facebook Ads that get results and more clients.

Here is what you are going to learn in this chapter, you're going to learn what not to do with your Facebook Ads. And this is probably what you've been doing, let's be honest. I'm going to tell you not to do it.

I'm going to tell you how to make authentic connections with people on Facebook and turn them into sales and new clients in your business. I'll also share strategies to build your business for the long term, not just wasting money now on ads.

So, who am I? I'm Delight Iverson. My website is marketingwithdelight.com. I am also a wellness professional like you. I am a certified Reiki master. I do some healing work as well as some intuitive work. Then I became a Facebook Ads Expert.

I started doing Facebook Ads for my own business, then I got so good at it, and I saw so many people in our industry just wasting their money and getting nowhere with their ads, that I decided to help out.

Now, that has just taken over my business, so I like to mix in my crunchy, healing, spiritual energy into doing Facebook Ads.

I manage ads for clients. I could take over their entire ads strategy and do everything day to day. I also teach business owners to DIY their ads, which is my favorite thing to do.

I live in Colorado; I love snowboarding and my dog. This is kind of a key; I'm sharing this with you strategically because those are the things that I share on my Instagram and my Facebook to connect with my future clients. I like to share a little bit about my pets and my hobbies, I do that on purpose. So, if you want to check that out, it's @marketingwithdelight on Facebook and Instagram. All right. So, that's me.

Are you getting it wrong?

Here is where people get it wrong. They think about Facebook Ads the same way they think about an ad on TV or the radio. They create a special promotion, and they blast it out to everybody within a 25 or 50-mile radius of their office. Or they boost posts that tell people to buy buy buy. Like, "Come to my office, book an appointment, I can do this for you." Or, they waste their money even more by doing a promotion. They promote their page for more likes.

So, if you have used Facebook for business, you have seen where they're always trying to get you to do this, they pop this little blue button that says, promote your page. No, don't ever do that. No.

Okay, I want you to remember this as we get into this presentation, DABS, "don't always be selling." That's not what Facebook Ads are for actually. Facebook is a totally different medium than the type of ads you see on TV, or billboards, or radio. You've got to have a different strategy because it's a different type of medium.

On Facebook, it's all about the audience. People don't get on Facebook to book wellness appointments. They don't get on Facebook to go, "I wonder if I could find a massage therapist." They go on Google if they want to do that.

The reason they're on Facebook is to chat with their friends, argue about politics and watch cat videos and maybe stalk an ex-boyfriend or girlfriend, who knows. Okay? Let's be honest. So, that's the audience that you're dealing with.

They're distracted, they're not looking for you, and those are the people who are going to see your ads. It sounds like, oh God, how does this ever work? But, here is how it works because 90% of the time, you aren't going to sell anything with your Facebook Ad. You're not going to be selling stuff.

You are going to be doing two things, most of your budget, your time and your energy is going to go to goal number one, which is building your warm audiences. I'm going to talk more about exactly what a warm audience is in a minute.

Then number two, which is obviously important, but you're not going to need to spend that much time, and energy on this part is retargeting all of those warm audience with a sales ad.

Those are the two types of ads that work really well for wellness professionals, and I'm going to go over this with you and the strategy behind this.

Again, I have to hit this because I just think this is such a waste especially in 2018. This is like a 2008 strategy, okay? Your goal is not to get likes for your page or promote your page as Facebook will call it sometimes. This will happen naturally as you do more ads, which is great because it's nice to have likes for your page because it shows social proof. It shows that you're established, but it's just not the most important number for your business.

Likes don't pay you money; new clients pay you money. That's what you're going to invest in is getting new clients. And the likes will happen as you go.

Building your audience

Okay, so let's talk about the first type of ad, your audience building ad. Your goal with these audience building ads is to build up the know, like and trust factor.

Now, this is like a cliché that we always talk about in business, but it's so true. People want to buy services from people they know and like and trust. Especially when it's a wellness field, it could be a very intimate experience; whether it's a massage or acupuncture or Reiki or chiropractor or whatever, it's an intimate experience. It's really nice to know something about your practitioner before you have your first appointment.

Social media is the best way to help more people get to know you quickly and see if they like you and they like your energy, and they feel comfortable coming to you for help with their health; their mental, emotional, spiritual health.

You should be making videos

What type of content builds KLT, know, like and trust? Videos. So, I can hear people virtually groaning already. Yes, I think you should be making videos.

This is the best thing you could do, and not a lot of people are doing it because it's not easy, right? It's not easy for me to do this right now, to talk to you and create this presentation but guess what, I'm doing it and I'm making connections because of it. So, put on your big girl pants and your big boy pants and make some videos.

So, there are two different kinds you can do. One is Facebook Live, which I absolutely love doing. I do them every week over at my Marketing With Delight page. I talk about all these different types of topics over there. I love it because it's live. To me it feels like way less pressure when it's live because if I mess up or make a mistake, it's like, well, it's live. Everyone expects that. It's also just such a good way to connect with people and give them a little slice of your life.

It's actually great on a Facebook Live if your cat jumps up in your face like mine tends to do because it helps people get to know you and they see that you're human. And they're like, "Oh, I might be able to trust this person."

That's Facebook Live video; it's really great. Another one is pre-recorded. That's something if you're too nervous to do Facebook Live, which we all are when we start, and you want to try pre-recorded first, you can do that as well.

So, just record something with your iPhone and then upload it to Facebook and make a post with it that way. Both of those are good, but I really think Facebook Live is faster and easier and it helps people get to know you even better.

Topics

So, topics for your videos. One is a tour of your office. This could definitely be pre-recorded, but it would be cool to do it live as well and just talk to people around the office or see what happens.

Education about self-care. Giving people some quick tips about things they can do at home that relate to your specialty. One example that I want to give for this presentation, for me, I've had a lot of problems with TMJ. I clench and grind my teeth when I'm sleeping.

There is a lot that I've found helps me, acupuncture, Reiki, and chiropractic, they all help me with this because it's definitely stress related. It's not just a purely physical thing.

So, if you were trying to get someone like me to book with you, you would give a couple of tips about TMJ if you're a massage therapist or acupuncturist or if you practice any wellness modality that would help me with TMJ.

Giving a couple of tips about a specific issue people are having to help them at home, and then you can say, "And tip number three is, get yourself an acupuncture treatment." You've got to educate people because the majority of the popular don't know what you can do for them. I'm in this world, so I know, and I've taken advantage of these treatments, but not everybody knows that for example, acupuncture or chiropractic could help TMJ.

That's a great way to educate people about ways to take care of themselves at home, and then also coming to see you.

Talk about your philosophy. This sounds lofty maybe, but I'm always curious about that one. I met a massage therapist recently, and I just asked her, how does she feel about treating emotions through her massage? Is it purely physical, or does she work on an emotional level with people?

She talked to me about how she can sometimes feel emotions releasing from people or sometimes occasionally people will cry while they're on the table because they're just releasing emotions. So, things like that are what I mean about the philosophy of your work.

And then, this is the one I love. I don't think any of us do this enough because it feels like tooting your own horn, but we should be doing this more. Tell success stories of clients who you've helped with your services.

So, I come to you, I have a horrible TMJ, and you help me, and I feel better. Well, you can get on, do a quick Facebook Live and tell everybody about it. Or better yet, you could even interview me about it.

You can get your clients to agree to that if you have some people who aren't too shy to be on video, you can interview them about their experience with you and post that as a video.

That could be a really good one as well. There are lots of ideas. The sky is the limit here; these are just a couple of things to get you started.

Engaging your audience

Okay. So, aside from video, some other types of content if you really don't want to do video or if you're a good writer and you like writing, you could do some posts. And you want them to be engaging.

These are going to be image and text posts. So, as I mentioned before, you can do some personal posts, so people get to know you.

I post pictures of my dog; I post pictures of me snowboarding in the mountains in Colorado, that's like the lifestyle piece. I wouldn't say this should be more than 20% of your posts.

I don't want every single post to be of my dog even though he is adorable. I do want people to know about my Facebook Ads as well. But it's great to post some of these things occasionally to make yourself relatable and human and connect with people in that way.

Other types of engaging posts that are more business related is to ask your audience questions that relate to your services or niche to get them engaging in the comments.

This might take a little bit of brainstorming and some experimenting, but really, asking questions is something that Facebook wants and will push out your posts to more of your followers when you are asking them questions to get them to engage.

An example of this could be on TMJ for example like, have you ever struggled with TMJ, what helped you? I asked this once in a group I'm in with a bunch of healers, and I got so many comments just asking, "I have TMJ, what have you guys tried? Has anybody had this? What have you guys tried?" And holy cow, so many comments.

It just gets the topic started, and it's totally fine if people comment and they say things that aren't related to your service, that's okay. The point is to get people to comment, talk about their experiences.

That would be a cool way to start the conversation about TMJ, and then, of course, you're going to be offering them a great TMJ massage eventually or treatment later on.

You can also tell your success stories through a text and image post. You could take a picture of your client or use a stock photo and talk about your client who had this horrible TMJ and now is feeling so much better and is finally eating salad and is so happy.

Okay, so those are some types of posts that you can make to grow your audience on Facebook. All of these types of posts and this strategy builds your warm audience. That's people who know, like and trust you. And people who will make referrals to you maybe even if they don't come in right away, they might still be referring to you.

It will just help you to make real connections with real people. You'll be starting a dialogue especially by doing some of those question type posts, or if you're making a video, you can ask questions to your video viewers and say in the comments, "Have you ever had a problem with TMJ?" And ask people to comment.

When you're doing ads this way, you're not just screaming constantly about your business and your services; you're spending some money strategically to grow your connections on Facebook with people who would be interested once they get to know you. And you're reminding people about you and just keeping yourself top of mind for when they do need your services.

As you're doing these types of ads; you're building your warm audiences, then you get to do sales retargeting ads. This is where it gets sexy, and you get to do sales and make money.

Here is an example with the video view. So, let's keep talking about the TMJ example. Let's say you are a massage therapist and you make a video with some tips for self-care about TMJ.

At the end of the video, you are inviting people to come in for an appointment, but that's not the point, yet. You can mention it in the video, but you're not going to sell it hard, you're just going to be like, "Hey, I have an office downtown, and you can come in." Mostly that video is just going to be giving them some value, giving them some tips, letting them know you exist.

Next step, is you promote that video for more video views. There is a way to do this inside of Facebook; it's called a Video Views Campaign. This is not boosting. I don't believe you can hit boost and get more video views, which is unfortunate because video views are cheap.

If you do this right, you can get video views for one cent, two cents, three cents each. So, if you spend $10, you could get 50 to 100 views on your video.

So next point here, you can create an audience with all of the people who viewed your video for three seconds or more and then build an ad for a special on your TMJ massage for first-time clients. Maybe it's like $10 off, 15% off, I don't know what you want to do.

This doesn't even have to be a percentage off, it could be something else, but I just say a special price to give them some urgency or get them motivated to take action, but you can always play around with what that special offer is going to be for that massage or treatment.

The thing that's important to reiterate here is; you're targeting your ad for this TMJ massage special only to people who have watched your TMJ video. You are not blasting the entire tri-county area with an ad for this. So, you're going to save yourself money and aggravation. You're going to be connecting and making deeper relationships with people who really want to hear from you, and who are likely to buy from you versus just the spray and pray and hope for something to happen.

You put in a little bit of work, on the front end giving some value, helping people get to know you and then you offer them a special deal to get them to come into your office for the first time.

So, if you're doing video, or you could try both of these strategies, there is the page engagement example. You create that engaging post that gets comments. You're asking a question about TMJ. Maybe you're asking that question of, "If you suffered from TMJ, what helped you feel better?" Then you're finding out.

That's always great to find these things out from your audience because then you can talk about them. So, if a bunch of people is saying, "Oh, I take five Advil every day." Maybe, later on, you do a post about how Advil can burn a hole in your stomach. I'm exaggerating, I don't know the details, but I just know it's not very good!

So, you've got your people commenting; then you build a post-engagement campaign, so you're going to spend a little bit of money here to get this out to more people for more engagement.

Maybe these are people who don't follow your page yet but would be interested. Facebook will send it out to more people in your area for more post engagement. And once somebody likes, comments, or shares, then they go into your page engagement.

Then you're going to create this page engagement audience, and it's going to be like capturing all of these people who have been coming on to your page because of your post engagement campaign, okay?

This is building your audience, and then once you have a bigger audience, then you have your ad for your TMJ special, and you target all the people in your page engagement audience with that special.

It works a little more cleanly and directly when you do a video; it's another reason I love video so much because your page engagement audience isn't just people who comment on that one TMJ post. Your page engagement audience is going to be everybody who likes your page, who visits your page, who comments or likes or shares any of your other posts.

It could be people who comment on a picture of your dog, they could get the ad, but that's okay too. At least they know who you are. So, even if they don't have TMJ, maybe they know somebody who has TMJ. It's okay to do it that way too. I like the laser-focused way of doing it with a video about your topic, retargeting the video viewers with an ad.

Those are two ways to do it. There are a few steps there. It's a bit of a funnel experience where your customer, your new client is seeing you in some way where you're giving them value whether it's that they're engaging with you or they're watching your video. Then they see an ad from you for a service that's related to the video or post that they saw.

So, you're probably wondering, oh man; there are probably a few questions right now. One, how much is all of this going to cost? This is always a question that I get from people, how much do we need to spend? Let's look at this. With this strategy, you will actually save money, and you will get better results even though you're doing two types of ads, it's going to save you money, let me show you.

Here is an example budget from the old 2008 way where you just spray and pray. Actually, I'm not sure if we had Facebook Ads in 2008. Anyway, let's say you spend $100 blasting sales ads to everyone in your area; man, women, and child in the tri-state county area. And it's, "Come in for a TMJ massage. Get $10 off."

Your results, who knows, maybe you get some clicks through to your website, maybe you get a sale or two, it's possible. This sometimes works. Sometimes you get sales, but you're not getting any relationship building. You spend that $100, and if you don't have all these pieces in place to build those audiences so that you can keep retargeting them and keep connecting with them, then you just spend that money, and if you don't get any sales, it's like, "Oh man." It's just gone.

But this way, the 2018 way, also known as the Awesome Strategy, let's say you spend, this is just an estimate here. Let's say you spend $85 growing your warm audience with a video views campaign, or a post-engagement campaign if you don't do video.

Then, you spend $15 on a sales retargeting ad to those video viewers. The reason why you can spend so little in those retargeting ads is that your audience is really small compared to the whole tri-county area, versus all the people who watch your video.

But if you do it right and you spend $85 on your video, you could get hundreds of people in that audience with $85 to then re-target with your $15. But it's not the same as if you're just blasting out that sales ad to your whole area.

It depends where you live, but you might have hundreds of thousands of people or even a million people on that audience. You need to spend way more money to reach people.

Hopefully, that makes sense how I'm explaining it there. Your results here, the worst case scenario is, you grow your audience and invest in your future because if you spend $85 on video views, those people will watch your video and they will get into your video views audience, and you can keep going from there.

The next time you make a video, you can target those people again so that they see you again, and then some of them will like your page, and some of them will start moving forward with you, and they'll comment and all of that.

That's the worst-case scenario. The best case scenario is people will book, and you get new clients, and you make money. Now, that doesn't always happen the very first time. That's something I'm going to get to here in a minute. With patience and testing, the best case will definitely happen for you. There's absolutely no reason why this wouldn't get you sales after maybe a couple of tries. It definitely could work on the very first try. Or it might be that you need to test a little bit to tighten up your offer. Maybe it's $10 off; maybe it's 15% off.

It's all about figuring out how to package that special offer for new clients. It might need some tweaking and testing and things like that.

One last note about your budget. I just gave you an example of spending $100; this is worth testing out with $100. Of course, you can spend more, but don't bother if you don't have $100 to spend.

I hear people talking about wanting to do Facebook Ads, and I feel like they don't want to spend any money. But you're advertising; you have to spend money.

Facebook Ads are not free, they are Facebook Ads, right? Wrap your mind around spending at least $100 to test. If you don't get a client right away, that has to be okay with you.

Don't spend your last $100 on this. It's too risky. You don't want to put yourself in this high-pressure situation because that vibe comes through.

You try to make a video and do all the strategies I'm talking about, and it's so much pressure, you're like, "Oh my God, I can't pay my rent. This better work." Terrible energy, don't do it. Don't do it that way.

If that's where you're at in your business, you probably just need to do some hustling and wait on Facebook Ads until you have some money to invest. You might not get a return right away, give it 90 days.

Only invest as much as you feel comfortable, don't expect a return in that same month.

I think that if you spend $100 a month for three months, you should be getting new clients within 90 days with this strategy. It can happen faster if you want to spend a little bit more. But 90 days is a reasonable amount of time. Just don't stress yourself out with your budget and feeling pressure to need a return right away.

Now, your other question, how do I do all of this? If you're understanding and you're following my strategy here where you're making a video, you're doing the video views campaign. You're making an audience of the video viewers, and you're making an ad to the viewers, how do you do all of that? It is unfortunately not that intuitive inside of Facebook Ads.

You're going to need some training to do this properly, to not waste your time and money. I have a program for you I'd like to invite you to consider, it's called Better Boosting.

I've been talking about how I hate when people boost, boosting is not a good plan; it's just very inefficient. It's very spray and pray. This is Better Boosting, where we're going to go through exactly how step by step by step with video tutorials to show you how to do this inside of the Facebook Ads Manager.

You're going to learn exactly what I've been talking about, how to execute the strategies I've been talking about here today. You're going to learn how to build your warm audiences. You're going to learn how to do those video views campaigns and or post engagement campaigns.

Then you're going to learn how to build your audience library. There is five main type of audiences that you're going to want to target with your Facebook Ads. Two of them we talked about today, video views and warm audiences. You're going to learn exactly how to set all of those up inside of Better Boosting. And you're also going to learn to create look-alikes to reach more people just like your hottest prospects.

This is so super cool. This takes away the mystery of what you're going to do to target your ads to grow your audience. You're going to use look-alike audiences to find more people like your best people.

Then you're going to learn how to set up those sales and retargeting ads. You're going to need to learn how to build out all three levels of your ads to maximize the exposure to those warm audiences.

You're going to learn about your budget a little more in-depth than I went here in this chapter. So you know what to expect and what to spend.

You're going to learn about timing, how to make it all work in the correct amount of time. And some tips for creative, like the copy, it's the text in your ad, and the image tips and things like that so that you have the best ad possible and you're showing up well on Facebook to these people you've built a relationship with.

You can learn more, if this sounds good to you, if you'd like to learn how to execute all of this, I walk you through it step by step by step. You can go to marketingwithdelight.com/better-boosting and learn more about that program and how it all works. It's very affordable. I think it should be well within your budget.

If you're ready for Facebook Ads, and you have some money to invest in ads and education, you don't want to start doing ads without getting some training. As I said, it's not intuitive; it's not easy. It's complicated, but it's going to be so worth it.

You can get some amazing results with these ads especially because people in this industry are not doing this. This is very outside the box.

This is pretty cutting edge, and you're going to stand out from the rest by doing this. And you're going to find your dream clients, and it's going to be great.

I would love to help you move forward with that. Go to marketingwithdelight.com/better-boosting. I'd love to see you there and have a great day.

Meet Your Hosts

Tim Cooper

Tim Cooper is a Remedial Massage Therapist, coach, author, podcaster, and educator.

Before studying massage in 2003, Tim worked as a software design engineer and business analyst for over 20 years.

In 2013 Tim completed his first marketing course and fell in love with the science of marketing and social psychology.

Tim brings a unique blend of industry, technical and business knowledge to his coaching clients and students around the world.

Gael Wood

Gael Wood is a Massage Therapist and Esthetician with over 22 years of business experience.

She now helps therapists all over the world learn to market their businesses on a budget using content marketing, local networking, and creating marketing materials that attract ideal clients.

She loves to share her enthusiasm for making business promotion fun and creative.

Global Wellness Professionals Marketing Summit

Tim and Gael are passionate about the wellness industry and seeing wellness professionals succeed. That's why the Global Wellness Professionals Marketing Summit was born! To help massage therapists, acupuncturists, chiropractors, naturopaths, homeopaths, Reiki healers, energy healers, Bowen therapists, spa owners… everybody involved in the health and wellness industry to prosper.

Right now people are spending three times more on natural health and wellness than conventional medicine. Now is YOUR time to shine. You just need a roadmap, time proven and tested strategies to get you there and keep you there.

Here's your free gift to help get you started!

globalwellnessprofessionalsmarketingsummit.com/messenger-bot

One Last Thing…

If you enjoyed this book or received value from it in any way, then we'd like to ask you for a favor: would you be kind enough to leave a review for this book on Amazon? It'd be greatly appreciated!

Please leave a review at gwpms.com/vsp-review

www.ingramcontent.com/pod-product-compliance
Lightning Source LLC
Chambersburg PA
CBHW070605220526
45467CB00003B/1311